The Complete Guide to

Irish Dance

First published in 2000
by Appletree
The Old Potato Station
14 Howard Street South
Belfast BT7 1AP

Tel: +44 (0) 28 90 243074
Fax: +44 (0) 28 90 246756
Web Site: www.appletree.ie
E-mail: reception@appletree.ie

The Complete Guide To Irish Dance

A catalogue record for this book is
available from the British Library

ISBN 0-86281-805-2

9 8 7 6 5 4 3 2 1

The Complete Guide to

Irish Dance

Frank Whelan

APPLETREE

CONTENTS

Part 1

History of Irish Dance   8

Types of Irish Dance   24

Irish Dancing Today   30

Irish Dancing Costumes   37

Cultural Organisations and Dance in Ireland   43

Music in Ireland   49

A Tribute to Teachers   61

Part 2 – A Selection of Thirty Popular Irish Competition and Social Dances

Guide to Dance Formations   67

Explanation of Common Terminology and Often Used Movements   68

Instructions for Hand and Arm Positions   71

Instructions for Steps   73

Two-Hand Jig   85

Two-Hand Reel   88

Stack of Barley   90

An Rince Mór   91

Bonfire Dance   94

Rince Fada   98

Bridge of Athlone   101

Haste to the Wedding   104

Siege of Carrick   107

Antrim Reel	110
Waves of Tory	114
Rakes of Mallow	119
Walls of Limerick	121
Siege of Ennis	123
Four-Hand Reel	125
Humours of Bandon	130
Harvest-Time Jig	134
Fairy Reel	138
Clencar Reel	142
Duke Reel	146
Cross Reel	150
Sweets of May	154
Eight-Hand Reel	158
High Caul Cap	162
Eight-Hand Jig	166
Three Tunes	171
Morris Reel	176
Haymakers Jig	179
Lannigan's Ball	181
Sixteen-Hand Reel	184

PART 1

History of Irish Dance

Early History

While there is no record in ancient Irish literature of the development of dance, it is difficult to believe that a race such as the ancient Irish, well known for their love of music, never danced. The absence in Ireland of such dances, as practised by the British and continental Celts who shared similar cultures to the Irish at that time, would be remarkable. It would also be strange if a people with a native taste for music, as is evident by the great number of musical instruments they possessed, had no knowledge of dancing, as dancing normally preceded music. We must presume that the development of man in Ireland was no different than the development of the human race around the world.

In every stage of man's development, from a primitive savage hunting and gathering food as he wandered through vast forests, to his present mechanically aided multimedia, Internet, e-mail and digital existence, he has performed dance. In earlier times the dances were simple, but as he learnt to control his environment by different work techniques, he changed the conditions in which he lived. His dances became more complicated. To trace the evolution of dance accurately is impossible, as different parts of the world have gone through various stages of development at different times.

They are roughly classified as follows:

Lower Hunters – food gatherers and hunters with spears.

Higher Hunters – these used the bow and arrow and made the first attempts to domesticate animals.

Pastoral – two stages: cattle-raising and limited agriculture.

Agricultural – the hoe is superseded by the plough and then the tractor.

In Ireland we have quite good evidence of this development from approximately 3000 BC thanks to the Neolithic burial chambers (passage graves) in the Boyne Valley, Newgrange, Knowth, and Dowth in County Meath, and the great archaeological work carried out in recent times.

The different types of dance performed in ancient times would have been tree worship dances, animal dances, work dances, war dances, courtship dances and recreational dances.

The first music is said to have been brought to Ireland around 1600 BC by the Tuatha De Danann (meaning the skilled workers) who were believed to have come from the region surrounding the River Elbe in Germany. They were fair-haired, very energetic and, according to tradition, a very cultured people. It was from a De Danann queen named Erin that Ireland derived one of its names. In 1300 BC, when Ollam Fodhla was king, the first great feis was held at Tara called Feis Teamhair, meaning House of Music.

The Celts, or Keltoi, came to Ireland approximately 500 BC. Their language and culture was firmly established by the early Christian era. With the Christianization of Ireland and the coming of St Patrick (approximately AD 431), successful attempts were made to put a Christian image to the pagan dances and rituals, but the basic pagan movements were maintained.

The first small Viking raids on Ireland occurred in AD 795 and the raids continued until the ninth century by which time the Viking settlers had substantially influenced Irish culture. The invaders were mainly Norwegian in origin and were known as the Fingaill (the fair foreigners) as distinct from the smaller number of Danish settlers, known as the Dubhgaill (the dark foreigners). By the middle of the ninth century a population group known as the Gall-Gaidil (Norse-Irish) was identified. Settlement, intermarriage and the sharing of each other's way of life encouraged cultural and linguistic assimilation. In reality their involvement with Ireland lasted almost 400 years and their influence is felt to this day.

Following the Anglo-Norman invasion (1169–72), the Normans are given credit for having introduced round dances to Ireland in the twelfth century. The round dances had become a favourite pastime of the French nobility and about the time of the Norman invasion of Ireland these dances were very popular in Normandy. There can be little doubt that these dances were performed in the Norman strongholds and towns in Ireland.

When the mayor of Waterford visited O'Driscoll of Baltimore in 1413, carolling is said to have taken place. Carolling was a mixture of singing and dancing which was popular with the Normans at that time and was still being performed well into the late twentieth century in some parts of Wexford. In 1443, 2,700 people participated in the first great Festival of Arts, which was held on 26 March at Killeigh and included music, dance and poetry.

After much searching of early Irish literature by several authors for reference to Irish dancing (O'Curry, 1873; O'Keeffe and O'Brien, 1902; Joyce, 1903, etc.), they were unsuccessful except for three words translated from Irish into Latin to describe Salome dancing before Herod: 'cleasaí   ocht', 'léimneacht' and 'hopaireacht'; none of these words were in common usage in Ireland.

In the modern language the two words used to describe dancing ('damhsa' and 'rince') are borrowed from other countries. 'Damhsa' is derived from the French word 'danse' or its English equivalent 'dance', and the earliest use of the word in the written language dates only from around 1520. 'Rince' is a borrowing of the English word 'rink', meaning to skate on ice. The words 'cor' and 'port', which we use today to describe reels and jigs, do not properly signify these dances but are meant to describe quick lively pieces on the harp. 'Jigeánnai' and 'rileánna' are borrowings from the English. The word 'jigeánnai' derives from the Italian word 'giga', an old dance. 'Reel' is derived from the Anglo-Saxon word 'rulla' meaning to whirl. There is also a suggestion that the word 'reel' comes from the Swedish word 'ragla' which means to stagger, incline or move in walking, first to one side and then the other.

In sixteenth- and seventeenth-century Anglo-Irish and English literature we find several references to Irish dances. The dances in question were usually called roundelays, heys, trenchmores, jigs and rince fada. In a 1549 Scottish publication, 'Complainte of Scotland', there is reference to the ring dance of Scotland being very similar to the rince fada or field dance of the Irish.

In Grattan Flood's book, History of Irish Music (1905), there is reference to a letter sent to Queen Elizabeth I written by Sir Henry Sidney in 1569 in which he writes about the ladies of Galway dancing Irish jigs and said to be magnificently dressed, very beautiful and first-class dancers. It is most probable that the jigs referred to were group jigs and not solo jigs, as the solo dancing did not appear until much later.

It would appear that some of the country dances then in vogue in Ireland had been superseded in England by French dances, and had been completely forgotten in that country. Spenser, in his View of Ireland (1596), refers to the old manner of dancing among the Irish as owing its origin to the original inhabitants, then believed to have come from Scythia on the shores of the Black Sea. In fact, country dancing spread from England into Ireland.

In 1600 Fynes Moryson, Secretary to Mountjoy during the latter's term of office in Ireland, describes the manners and customs of the natives:

The Irish delight much in dancing but only in country dances ... whereof they have some pleasant to behold, as Balrudery, and the Whip of Dunboyne, and they dance about a fire in the midst of a room holding sticks in their hands and by certain strains drawing one another into the fire; and this I have seen them often dance before the Lord Deputy in the houses of Irish lords.

Mention of the jig being danced in Ireland occurs in 1674. Dr Talbot, Archbishop of Dublin, caustically refers to the life being led by Friar Peter Walsh and his followers as being one of good cheer and dancing jigs and country dances.

In his Voyage through the Kingdom of Ireland in 1681, Dineley mentions that the Irish on holidays are much addicted to dance 'after their country fashion, that is the long dance one after the other of all conditions masters, mistresses and servants'. From this report we can conclude that the long dance, the rince fada, was popular with all classes of society.

When King James II landed at Kinsale, County Cork, in March 1689, at that time we are told that 'all along the road the country came to meet his majesty … orations of welcome being made unto him at the entrance of each considerable town and young rural maidens weaving dances before him as he travelled.'

A later account (*c.* 1780) tells us that he was welcomed on his arrival at the seashore in Kinsale with the 'rinceadh-fada', the figure and execution of which delighted him exceedingly. The dance, we are told, was performed by three persons moving abreast, each of whom held the end of a white handkerchief. They advanced to slow music, and were followed by the rest of the dancers in pairs, each of which held a white handkerchief between them.

The popularity of dancing in the seventeenth and eighteenth centuries has been mentioned in the writings of several travellers throughout Ireland. Richard Head in one of his works entitled The Western Wonder (1674) says of the Sunday amusements: '… in every field a fiddle and the lasses footing it till they are all of a foam'. Dances mentioned in seventeenth-century literature include the Withy Dance, the Sword Dance, the War Dance and the Long Dance.

Arthur Young, noted English agriculturist and traveller, notes in his tour of Ireland (1776–9) that 'dancing is very general among the poor people. Almost universal in every cabin. Dancing masters of their own rank travel through the country from cabin to cabin. Weddings are always celebrated with much dancing.'

There is an account of a May Eve Dance in Athy, County Kildare, in 1787 when twenty-four couples, young men and women, dressed in white and ornamented with ribbons, engaged in a dance which was performed in a space over a quarter of a mile in length. At one end a maypole was erected, and the other end a large bonfire was lit. The dance involved two hobby horses, and several bladders tied to a long staff. In 1803 we are told 'this dance is still practised on rejoicing occasions in Ireland'.

John Carr, in his Stranger in Ireland (1805) states: 'A Sunday with the peasantry in Ireland is not unlike the same day in France. After the hours of devotion, a spirit of gaiety shines upon every hour, the bagpipe is heard, and every foot is in motion.'

The Old Irish Dancing Masters

The biggest influence on Irish dancing was the dancing master who appeared on the social scene in Ireland in the second half of the eighteenth century. He was the person who shaped the future of Irish dance by introducing refinement and discipline in the group dances and cultivating and developing the footwork of the solo dances. With the coming of the dancing master, Irish dancing reached the height of its perfection in the solo or step dances.

Arthur Young noted that dancing was very popular amongst the people. He wrote: 'All the poor people, both men and women, learn to dance and are exceedingly fond of the amusement.' Dancing masters travelled throughout the country staying from nine days to six weeks in one location. They were always accompanied by a piper or fiddler.

The dancing master was a somewhat whimsical figure, pretentious in dress and affecting a grandiloquence not sustained by his schooling. He wore a Caroline hat, swallow-tailed coat, tight knee breeches, white stockings and turn-pumps, and carried a cane with a silver head and silk tassel. Dressed in this fashion we can presume that the dancing master was of higher standing than the fiddler or piper; he was a person to be treated with respect by all in the local community and especially his pupils. He prided himself on his good carriage and deportment which he endeavoured to pass on to his pupils. He considered himself a gentleman and behaved like one.

His coming to a community was an occasion of great delight. On arrival the dancing master would arrange with a farmer for the loan of a building or barn to use as his base for teaching dance and also often stayed with the farmer if he had space in the house or barn – in return he would give free lessons to the children of the farmer. Sometimes if the farmer had no room the pupils would take turns in taking the master home for the night.

The first steps the pupils were taught were the rising step of the jig and the side step of the reel. There are references to dancing masters having to resort to fixing sugar and straw to their pupils' feet to enable them to distinguish the left foot from the right! Jingles were used to impart the rhythm of the step, for example: 'Rise upon sugar, sit upon straw.'

The dancing master was also engaged to teach deportment and other forms of court dances to the children of the well-to-do. Many dancing masters were also teachers of fencing, and fencing schools were often as common as the dancing schools. According to Arthur Young the fee charged was sixpence. In Wexford around 1816 pupils had to pay the master a 'thirteen' (there were thirteen Irish pence in a British shilling) and pay a 'tester' (sixpence-halfpenny) to the musician for a quarter of nine nights. With most dancing masters the quarter was more commonly six weeks. Towards the middle of the nineteenth century the charge was ten shillings per quarter for the dancing master and five shillings for the musician. During his stay in a community he would organise one or two benefit nights which were open to one and all; pupils were admitted free and a collection was usually made for the dancing master and musician.

The dancing master was usually a bachelor, having no fixed residence but travelling from house to house within a radius of twenty miles. He was not only famous for his dancing ability but also for his ability to compose steps; the art of composing new steps was a skill carefully guarded by the dancing master. Even up to the present day the status of dancing teachers is often judged by their ability to compose new steps of an acceptably high standard. Steps composed in the early days of the dancing masters were much fewer than they are today. Frequently when a dancing master composed a step, he would put his own name on the step, for example, Kelly's Number 5 or Murphy's Reel Number 1. Some of the steps composed in earlier times were easy enough to be written down, which is not often done today.

A dancing master from Kerry called O'Kearin was very famous at this time and it is he who is attributed with having brought order, uniformity and style to the steps being performed throughout Ireland. This was a mighty task and would be very difficult even in modern times.

Jerry Molyneaux from Kerry is said to be the last of the old-type dancing masters. He learnt his dancing from Batt Walsh who in turn learnt from Moor (known as Morrin) who was teaching in 1820.

The old dancing masters survived into the early twentieth century and to some of them in particular we owe the recovery of many of our figure dances.

O'Keeffe and O'Brian, authors of A Hand Book of Irish Dances (1902), the standard work on the subject, obtained a number of dances from:

Patrick (Professor) Reidy who had learnt his dancing from his own father, who had in turn been a pupil of the great dancing master O'Kearin, an old Kerry dancing master from Castleisland then living in London. These were the rince fada; the 4- and 8-hand reels; The High Caul Cap, St Patrick's Day 8-hand jig.

Tadgh Sean O'Sullivan, a dancing master from Glenbeigh, County Kerry: the 12- and 16-hand reels; the half chain 8-hand reel; Glenbeigh Bridge 8-hand jig; the Humours of Bandon 4-hand jig.

John O'Reilly of Killorglin, County Kerry: Cross Reel 8-hand reel; full chain 8-hand jig. Richard Foley of Knockmonlea, County Cork: Long (Big) Road reel; 4-hand reel.

Thomas Danaher of Moonegay, County Limerick: The Walls of Limerick (then known as The Limerick Walls); Long progressive dance.

Dances were collected in most parts of Ireland especially the North, where three of the most interesting dances were collected by Nan Quinn from Bessbrook, County Armagh and passed on to that great man of Irish dancing, Tom Farrelly from Dundalk. These were The Trip to the Cottage, The Sweets of May and The Three Tunes.

Each of these dances had something different from most other ceili dances – The Three Tunes is the only ceili dance to have a change in tempo and tunes, and it and The Sweets of May are the only ceili dances to involve actions with the exception of The High Caul Cap which has limited actions. The Trip to the Cottage does not commence with the usual type of 'lead around' and differs in construction to most of the dances in the Irish Dance Commission books.

The big influence these travelling dancing masters have had on the fostering and development of Irish dance over a 200-year period could not be emphasised enough. To them we owe the very existence of Irish solo and figure dances. Through their enthusiasm and dedication in good times and bad, they laid a great foundation for Irish dancing as we know it today.

The Church and Dancing in Ireland

The Church has had great influence on dance in Ireland since the seventeenth century. Records show that at almost no time was its hierarchy in favour of gatherings where people of both sexes participated in leisure-time activities which included dance. Women who participated in dance gatherings were condemned as being evil and enemies of the Lord.

These objections to gatherings of mixed sexes for the purpose of dancing were still very much the policy of the Church well into the middle of the twentieth century. One must only go back to the late fifties and early sixties when women were not allowed to drink in bars and lounges. They had to use the snug, which could be found in almost every pub and was usually not much bigger than a confession box, at most accommodating only three people. The policy was: a woman's place was in the home.

Attending Irish dance lessons, competitions and exhibitions was never any great problem as far as the clergy were concerned. I was told by several priests that when Irish dance groups travelled to international festivals abroad they usually had one or two priests as spiritual directors. The priests I spoke with had been on such trips. It was also the policy up to the late 1960s not to allow Irish dance groups to go to eastern European countries because in the eyes of the clergy countries such as Poland, Czechoslovakia, Estonia, Latvia and Lithuania were all anti-Christian. I had the privilege to visit these countries in 1968 and every year since, and in my opinion the people I met were very fine, honest Christians. It would appear it was just ignorance and a lack of understanding on behalf of some Irish people that led to these narrow views.

Today in Ireland the priests and bishops are not the only ones with a good education. We have a well-educated population who can think for themselves and are quite capable of knowing what is right and wrong – people are free to express themselves in music, song and dance. Women have long been liberated and are no longer confined to the house. It would not be unusual for some women to go to dance sessions several times a week and often travel some distance for weekend workshops.

While some priests and Christian Brothers took an interest in Irish dancing in the latter part of the twentieth century, the majority I knew had a very narrow view of dance and were more interested in it for political reasons rather than for the physical exercise and social pleasure which could be achieved by those who participated in it.

One of many priests I knew who was genuinely interested in Irish music and dance was Father Pat Aherne from County Kerry. In the late 1960s he founded one of the greatest Irish cultural experiences one could ever hope to enjoy – Siamsa Tíre, The National Folk Theatre in Tralee, which had a cast of twenty-seven. Their ages ranged from 11 to 60 and all of them could sing and dance. Father Pat also produced and presented Irish traditional folk art on stage in a very professional and creative way using the most modern stage lighting and sound effects. He lectured throughout Ireland at courses and workshops which were organised for producers and practitioners in the presentation of traditional folk art and culture. Father Pat dedicated his life to The National Folk Theatre and contributed greatly to the development and preservation of storytelling, music, song, dance and Irish folklore in the sixties and seventies at a time when most Irish traditional cultural organisations were only starting to develop.

Some Views of the Clergy

The following is a brief look at the relationship between the clergy and Irish dance and some of the views expressed by them in recent centuries.

In 1670 a priest in West Cork in the south of Ireland wrote: 'Women dancers are the cause of many evils, because it is they who bear arms in the devil's army. The devil compels them to gather on holidays for dancing, a thing which leads them to bad thoughts and evil actions.'

Dr Plunket, Catholic Bishop of Meath, in his sermon at Drumonrath in July 1790, condemned the promiscuous assembly of both sexes on Sundays for the purpose of dancing.

Father John Casey (1769–1861), parish priest in Ferriter, County Kerry, was a deadly enemy of music, dancing and pipe playing. He forbade pipers to play for dancers even though this was their sole source of income – without this, pipers were sentenced to a life of destitution and many died in the poor house. On another occasion Father Casey, finding a piper playing for dancers, kicked, cuffed and beat him unmercifully, breaking his pipes. The locals had to make a collection for the piper.

Waltzes and polkas were singled out by Pope Pius IX in 1864 as both these dances involved constant physical contact between couples and because they were fairly lively, with dancers seeming to enjoy themselves. As we all know, everything was fine with the Church as long as you did not take pleasure from it.

In 1875 the bishops of Ireland issued a pastoral address in which they denounced the improper dances which had been imported from abroad, clearly an occasion of sin.

In 1919 a piper called Ruane, in Teach an Gheta, having been told that the priest for no apparent reason had banned any further music, burst out crying, turned on his heel and went home. Ruane never came to another Sunday there – nor did any other piper.

The Archbishop of Dublin warned in 1923 that 'Dancing had become a grave danger to the morals of young people.'

Dr O'Doherty, when Bishop of Galway in 1924, said that 'The dances indulged in were not clean, healthy Irish dances.' (He seemed to forget that the same clean, healthy Irish dances he referred to had been stopped and almost wiped out by his predecessors.) The bishop went on to tell parents, 'Fathers of this parish, if your girls do not obey you, lay the lash upon their backs.'

In an address issued after their meeting in Maynooth College in October 1925, the archbishop and bishops of Ireland expressed the fear that the honour of Irish boys and the Christian modesty of Irish maidens that had been won for Ireland might be lost: '… dance halls, more especially in the general uncontrol of recent years, have deplorably aggravated the ruin of virtue due to ordinary human weakness.'

My father told me numerous stories of the priest walking the roads at night or hiding in the bushes – when a boy and girl came walking by he would pounce out and beat the lad with the stick and send him in the opposite direction of the girl.

I have heard many such stories including the one of the parish priest who was so against dancing and music that he used to prowl the country lanes at night in order to put a stop to these social gatherings which led to the occasion of sin. When he came upon a house dance he would storm in the door and proceed to scatter the dancers with his blackthorn stick, beating the musician and often putting his instrument into the fire. The boys would also get a good belt of the stick, and the girls would be marched home to their fathers who were encouraged to put the fear of God into them with a few lashes of the belt. The priest, having performed his so-called godly duty, would then use his most powerful weapon of intimidation and fear – the denouncing of the dancers and musician to all the parish from the altar at Sunday Mass.

This policy of the clergy contributed to the gradual disappearance of house dances, crossroad ceilis and many other Irish cultural activities. In turn this meant that musicians, not being able to find any work, had to emigrate to England, America and other countries with strong Irish communities where their talents would be appreciated. Ireland's cultural life was certainly the poorer for their leaving.

After very strong pressure from the clergy, the State introduced The Public Dance Halls Act of 1935, which forbade the holding of dances without a licence in buildings, yards, gardens or other enclosed places whether roofed or not, temporary or permanent. This law had the effect of almost wiping out informal social gatherings and did serious damage to the preservation and development of Irish dance.

On the Great Blaskets in 1936, Eibhlis Ní Súilleabháin wrote: 'Great changes have come on the Island lately, with the visit of two Redemptorists Fathers … no mixed bathing is allowed … no dancing in any house, day or night, no one out later than 10.30 pm.'

While today we may read these old laws and sermons against music, dance and social gatherings with much amusement, in their day they had to be taken very seriously. To go against the clergy could mean the blacking of an individual in the community and the refusal by the parish priest to give a reference, which was the practice in those days when it was time to leave the parish to seek work.

The Gaelic League

Throughout the nineteenth century a very strong movement was developing towards a national Irish identity, and this led to the founding of the Gaelic League in 1893. This organisation was to have a big influence in the future of Irish dance and today there are several thousand qualified teachers throughout the world. The Gaelic League is an Irish cultural organisation and had as its priority the promotion and preservation of the Irish language; it also promoted Irish dancing through both dancing classes and competitions. At the end of the nineteenth century the League sought to restore national identity and national pride, which at this time were at a very low ebb. The League had some of the country's top intellectuals as its founders and they wanted to establish a national identity to be proud of. Proper conduct, good behaviour and a certain amount of refinement were part of the new identity they were trying to create. (This was opposite to the uncultured, stage-Irish image which was too often portrayed around the world in those days.) The League developed very quickly and within a few years had thousands of members in Ireland, the USA and Great Britain. Hundreds of classes were organised in each country teaching dance and other forms of Irish culture.

The London branches of the Gaelic League were very active and progressive – they invented the ceili and introduced the term for such a dance gathering, and organised the first ceili, which was held in London in 1897. They have lots more to their credit, including the collection and preservation of the Irish figure dances (ceili dances). They also introduced the methodology and terminology to describe these dances, and these are still used today.

In the USA at the end of the nineteenth century, the League very quickly organised Irish dancing classes and competitions, and in a very short time was organising four big dancing competitions in four of the major cities each year.

In 1929 the Gaelic League set up a Commission of Inquiry to investigate the state of Irish dancing regarding teaching, classes, competitions and adjudication. This led to the Irish

Dance Commission being formerly set up in 1930, which continues to this day to supervise and organise the majority of Irish dancing around the world.

Social Factors and Irish Dance

When speaking about the development of Irish dance one must take into consideration many factors which have contributed to the changes in Irish dance as it has evolved over the centuries.

Up to the early twentieth century dance facilities were very restricted. Houses and living conditions were extremely cramped and had almost no space where people could dance – many houses had clay floors. The half-door was one solution, the table another; in pubs the tops of barrels were also used, and competitions were held on the backs of small lorries.

This lack of dancing space naturally had a very strong influence on the style of dance as movement would have been seriously restricted and, in some cases, people had to dance facing the one direction. Because of these restrictions one could presume that these dancers were not as physically developed as the solo dancers of today who cover such a large area on stage and perform some very athletic jumps and kicks which require hours of daily practice.

Clothing had a very important influence because in olden days the clothes were long and heavy. Women especially were very restricted because of their long dresses, shawls and whale-bone corsets. Not only were these heavy but they certainly made movement of the hands and feet very limited. Wearing such clothes was very tiring and the amount of time a dancer could dance was quite short.

Up to the beginning of the twentieth century a good pair of leather shoes was a very precious luxury. People used to walk to town in their bare feet and put on their shoes when entering the town. This certainly would have had an influence on poorer people learning hard shoe dances.

Mobility was a big problem and lack of transport confined most dancers to their own region, which in turn limited their knowledge of the standard of dancers from other areas.

As far as money was concerned, the majority of Irish people had just about enough to put food on the table for their family. Everything else was a luxury, and great sacrifices had to be made to get enough money to pay for dancing lessons, travel distances to competitions or buy dancing shoes and costume. Food (or the lack of it) would have had a serious effect on the physical development and stamina of a dancer.

And people – without people you cannot keep a folk culture and tradition alive. The majority of the young people in Ireland had to emigrate to look for work – they had no choice. And when the ordinary Irish person emigrated to America or England they very seldom returned. Musicians, singers and dancers departed in great numbers and this had a devastating effect on the living folk culture of Ireland.

Perhaps in places like Cork City in the south of Ireland there may have been more foreign influence on people's social lives, because of the fact that there were a great many British naval and military bases there. Cork Harbour was the main refuelling depot for the British Navy which also had several large bases, for example, at Fort Camden, Fort Carlisle, Spike Island and Halbowline. Altogether these bases would have had thousands of personnel permanently based in them. When one considers what a small city Cork is, the foreign influence must have been quite substantial, both culturally and economically.

Parts of the country which had British army barracks located nearby would also have been strongly influenced, as would areas which had their own Irish brigades (for example, the Connacht Rangers, who travelled all over the world and were stationed for long periods in many European countries). We must not forget that soldiers and sailors do not sit around when they have leave and they were the most constant travellers in and out of Ireland for hundreds of years. Can you imagine hundreds of soldiers returning to their barracks, say, in the West of Ireland, after being abroad for several years and having learnt a great many new folk dances from soldiers or locals in the different countries where they were stationed? Their influence would have been considerable.

Ulster

Special tribute must be made to the Irish dancing community in Ulster who produced some of the greatest solo and figure dance teams that Irish dancing has ever seen.

The Irish teachers and dancers from the North of Ireland had a special pride and commitment to their Irish dancing, perhaps more than in any other Irish dance community. The great Anna McCoy from Belfast had arguably the most famous Irish figure dance team in the twentieth century. The team was very much sought after for big events, concerts and television performances. Apart from 'Riverdance' no Irish dance group received so much publicity for Irish dance. The team were so professional in their performance that they often competed with other forms of dance on the famous BBC programme 'Come Dancing' and won. Once they took to the stage a great silence came over the hall and all eyes were focused on the stage. Other great Ulster teams were the Lillian O'More School and the Brendan de Glin School from Derry – between them they won dozens of All Ireland and World Dancing Championships. Unfortunately these great treasures of Irish Dancing were struck a very severe blow with the start of the troubles in Northern Ireland in 1969 – it was almost impossible for the dancers to attend their dancing classes because of the great danger involved. This led to an almost immediate collapse in the Irish dance structure in Ulster, bringing to an end the great era of Irish dancing there. We salute and sympathise with these lovers and protectors of Irish dance and culture – we hope that peace will come to their communities and soon the great Northern spirit will return to its rightful place at the forefront of Irish dancing.

Dancing and the Irish State

Funding

When it came to funding from the Arts Council, the government-appointed body to look after the arts, Irish dance has always being the poor relation. It was never looked on as an art form (or even as deserving mention) alongside other types of professional dance such as theatre dance, contemporary dance and community dance. These groups and companies get funding from the State but this is just enough to have one or two performances every year, with no real guarantee for their future. People who work as professional dancers or performers have to be admired for their courage and commitment to their art. As a member of the Dance Council of Ireland Board of Directors for eight years (four of them as President), I can say with good authority that the majority of the professional dance community in Ireland are very honourable hard-working people. I would be the first person to wish them more recognition and improvement in their conditions of employment – also much greater funding.

When we speak about Irish traditional dance we come into an area which has received almost no funding. Perhaps one of the reasons for this was because for years the Irish Dance Organisation (responsible for Irish dance) had a rule (the Ban) that any person who danced or participated in any other form of dance other than Irish would be expelled from the organisation. This showed a great lack of vision on behalf of the organisation whose main work was arranging competitions, implementing the rules and handing out suspensions.

One could easily understand how an Arts Council could never support an organisation which denied the young people of Ireland the freedom to broaden their minds by having an interest in other forms of dance and cultural life. Today the Ban is gone, but many of the people who enforced it are still around.

With the coming of 'Riverdance' it was to the benefit of many to go with the overwhelming flow of popularity and success that the show (and the others that followed) had achieved. Overall, there is now a much healthier respect for Irish dance – the 'Arty' people cannot close their eyes to the fact that Irish dance shows such as 'Riverdance' and 'Lord of the Dance' are the biggest dance performance success stories ever in Ireland (or indeed Europe) and would be highly rated at world level. And this was achieved, to the best of my knowledge, without state funding.

Today there is a more vibrant and healthy scene in the Irish dance world. The State are taking things more seriously and have a new Ministry for Arts, Culture and Heritage, which is much more sympathetic and open to all kinds of new ideas for folk culture and heritage projects.

Legislation

In 1935 the State enacted the Public Dance Halls Act which required that all public dances be licensed, including dances held in houses, yards, gardens, or other enclosed places. In the words of the Furrow, a journal published in Maynooth College, the act 'completely destroyed the informal dances in private houses which were a harmless and innocent way of country life'. This law effectively killed the house dances and did untold damage to the development and preservation of Irish dancing as a leisure-time activity.

Development of Irish Dancing Abroad

Irish dancing has developed in many countries including North America, Australia, New Zealand, England, Scotland, Wales, the Netherlands, South Africa, Argentina, anywhere the Irish have settled, you will find Irish dance activity.

USA

The USA has seen the biggest development of all countries. In a census carried out on 1 June 1890 there were more than four million children with both parents born in Ireland – this gives some idea of the great number of people of Irish descent living there. Irish dancing plays a very important role in the structure of Irish communities and helps preserve their identity. Although it has been taught informally since the middle of the nineteenth century, formal classes did not start until around 1900.

In Troy and Margaret West Kinney's book *The Dance* (1914), among the Irish dancers living in America was Thomas Hill, who was four times champion of Ireland (1909–10 and 1911 in Cork, and 1911 in Dublin). He was quoted as saying that thanks to the American Branch of the Gaelic League and its activity in the cause of arts, Irish dancing was in a flourishing condition. With an intelligent public interest, standards of excellence and a number of capable performers, America was now leading even Ireland. Thomas Hill attributed this to a combination of well-directed enthusiasm and the practice of holding four important competitions each year – these were divided among as many cities. Capable management attracted large numbers of good-class competitors and they were classified in such a way that there was hope for all. Liberality in prizes was an added stimulus. All told, Hill said, one feis accomplished as much interest in dancing as in Ireland in a year.

Between 1900 and 1950 there were very few certified teachers or adjudicators of Irish dancing. By 1967 there were seventeen teachers and five adjudicators. Today there are four hundred teachers and one hundred adjudicators, which is more than the number of qualified teachers in Ireland and England combined. The Healy School of Irish Dance from

San Francisco, which started classes in a formal manner in 1902, can boast four generations of teachers and will in 2002 celebrate its 100th anniversary.

Irish dancing has never been so popular. There are approximately 160 feiseanna (competitions) held throughout thirty states each year, and 2,000 dancers competed in the North American Championship. The approximate figure for Irish dancers attending classes is 50,000. Competitions are a way of life for Irish dancers – most travel by car, bus or plane almost every weekend to venues throughout the States. Many dancers such as Michael Flatley and Jean Butler of 'Riverdance' fame would have spent most of their young lives travelling each weekend to participate in competitions.

A large industry has developed to produce and sell Irish goods required by dancers such as costumes, shoes, socks, hairbands, brooches, records, tapes (audio and video), compact discs and books. Costumes can cost between IR£700 and IR£1,000.

The standard of North American dance in recent years has been of an extremely high level and the Americans are always a force to be reckoned with at the World Championships. Michael Flatley from Chicago was the first North American dancer to win the World Irish Dancing Championships.

Canada

While there had been a strong Irish dance community in the late nineteenth and early twentieth centuries, it is only in the last fifty years that Irish dance has been properly organised with registered teachers and examiners.

In 1947 an Irish dance teacher, Monica Dunne, arrived in Vancouver from Ireland. One of the biggest influences was Mae Butler, who was a well-known dancer and teacher in Ireland and came from County Dublin. Mae arrived in Toronto in 1953 and immediately set about putting a good structure for Irish dance in place. Today there are thirty qualified dancing teachers in Canada who attend the Mae Butler Academy of Dance. Irish dance in Canada is going from strength to strength thanks to the great work of the early pioneer teachers. Today Irish dancing is very popular and there are more than sixty registered teachers.

Australia

Earliest references to Irish dancing (taught mainly in Catholic schools) go back to the mid-nineteenth century, and the Queensland Championships were held between 1866 and 1900. It took a great many years to unite the different Irish dance associations into one organisation – the first examination under the auspices of The Irish Dance Commission for Teachers and Examiners took place in September 1969. At these exams thirty-two qualified as teachers and examiners (eighteen teachers, fourteen adjudicators). Today there are more than 150 registered teachers in Australia. In 1996 Conor Hayes became the first Australian man to win a World Championship.

New Zealand

The development and organisation of Irish dancing in New Zealand came at a later date than many other countries because there was not the large Irish population as in other countries. However, we understand that dancing existed during the time of the gold-rush days in Central Otago in the late nineteenth century. The first national organised competition was held in Christchurch in 1950. In 1972 two examiners from the Irish Dance Commission travelled to New Zealand to hold examinations and to provide refresher courses for those already qualified. There are approximately thirty registered teachers in New Zealand today.

England

The Irish community in England has always been to the front when it came to promoting and organising Irish dance and culture, because it was so important for them to maintain their identity and also to keep close links with their fellow Irish. The majority of the Irish workers in England had to work very hard to earn a living and to educate their families so that they would have a better chance in life. Great sacrifices were made by parents to take their children to dance competitions throughout England, to the All Ireland and, in more recent years, the World Championships.

The standard of Irish dance in England has always been equal to that in Ireland, and sometimes even better. Since the setting up and recording of formal competitions, you will always find a strong representation of the Irish dancers from England. Irish dance is very popular today and a large number of the professional dancers in 'Riverdance', 'Lord of the Dance' and many other shows are from England – children and grandchildren of families who sacrificed so much to promote Irish dancing in difficult times and circumstances. Today there are approximately 220 registered Irish dance teachers in England.

In many other countries you will find a great interest in Irish dance. Scotland has approximately thirty-six teachers, Wales three, the Netherlands one, and South Africa one. There are other countries, such as Germany, Sweden, Denmark, Norway, Finland, Belgium, France, the Czech Republic (to mention a few), who have today developed a great interest in Irish dance.

World Interest in Dance Courses

Every country around the world which has an Irish dance organisation is reporting an increasing interest in people learning Irish dance. There are also many dancers travelling to Ireland to participate in dance courses, including intensive courses with the Irish National Folk Company. They include solo and group dancers, and students from dance and physical education training schools. The courses they participate in offer a complete selection of Irish dance: solo, ceili, figure and group social set dance, as well as other aspects of Irish culture including tours to places of historical interest and ceilis. Dancers have come from Sweden, Germany, Holland, Hungary, Austria, Switzerland, the Czech Republic, France and

Denmark. Great interest has also been shown as far away as South Africa, Hong Kong, Japan, New Zealand, the USA and Canada. The more professional dance shows tour the world, the bigger the interest becomes.

The Influence of 'Riverdance' and 'Lord of the Dance'

The performance by Michael Flatley, Jean Butler and the others on the Eurovision Song Contest for a few minutes did more to promote Irish dancing around the world than had been achieved in the previous fifty years. So thanks to television, there came about the most important change in Irish dancing since the founding of dancing organisations. Irish dancing was treated with respect at home and abroad. Irish dancers could become professionals and make a career out of their hobby. Irish dancers now had something to aim for and after years of hard work and sacrifice they would be rewarded. They could travel to many parts of the world as respected entertainers. They could feel proud to be Irish.

There are now a number of Irish dance shows on tour worldwide including three or four 'Riverdance' shows. There are also several 'Lord of the Dance' shows and many others such as 'Feet of Fire' and 'Gaelforce Dance'. Unfortunately, there are some shows touring Europe which are not real Irish dance shows but just opportunists who are taking advantage of the success and publicity of the genuine ones.

There must be at least 600 professional Irish dancers making a living out of the great success of 'Riverdance' and other shows. The Irish dance scene has changed dramatically – Irish dancers are sought after for corporate and other events.

It is now very difficult to find young Irish dancers who are not focused on professional performance and benefits. Almost all available dancers are occupied in some show, cabaret or event. Moving into this level of show business has broadened the minds and talents of the dancers as they become aware of theatre lighting and sound and stage techniques, along with the discipline required to pace oneself for a full-time profession as a dancer.

The coming of 'Riverdance' has also changed much of the thinking regarding costume and movement. It has encouraged a more open and expressive form of dance with a greater freedom for the individual dancer.

How long these shows will continue to tour successfully, and what effect constant daily performance will have on the young dancers, remains to be seen. Only time will tell.

Types of Irish Dance

Solo Dances

Solo dancing was developed by the dancing masters in the last quarter of the eighteenth century and has since continued to develop in both a physical and artistic way. Today it expresses a great freedom of expression, an excellent posture, a true combination of brilliance, lightness and strength of movement, achieved by years of dedicated work.

Irish solo dancing as it exists today consists of the jig, the hornpipe, the reel and the set dance.

The Jig

As a solo dance the jig can be performed in different forms:

The Slip or Hop Jig is today only danced by women but until approximately 1950 was a competition dance for men and also couples. The slip jig, in 9/8 time, is a most graceful dance, performed in soft shoes, and is well highlighted in the spectacular dance show 'Riverdance'.

The Single Jig is at present performed as a light dance (with no trebling or sounds) in 6/8 and on rare occasions in 12/8 time.

The Double Jig can be danced either as a light dance with soft shoes (light jig) or as a heavy dance with hard shoes beating out the rhythm. Danced in hard shoes it is sometimes referred to as the Treble Jig, or the Heavy Jig or Double Jig, all of which are in 6/8 time.

The Heavy Jig is the only one of these which is danced in heavy (hard) shoes so the dancer can put emphasis on sound and rhythm.

The Hornpipe

The hornpipe almost certainly originated in England as far back as Elizabethan times when it was performed as a stage act, for example, the famous Sailors' Hornpipe.

The hornpipe as danced in Ireland is completely different and since the mid eighteenth century is played in 2/4 or 4/4 time. It is a hard shoe dance and is one of the most popular Irish dances throughout the world today.

The Reel

A very strong case can be made for ascribing a Scottish ancestry to our reels, as many can be attributed to known composers. The reel arrived across the water from our good neighbours and fellow Celts around 1800. It quickly became very popular and today it is the most popular Irish music and dance form. As soon as it arrived in Ireland it was transformed into what is now truly Irish and distinct from the Scottish reel dance.

Most reel steps are performed to double reel tunes, and single reel tunes are used for the more elementary steps for the novice or beginner. The reel is in 4/4 time and is danced in soft shoes.

The treble reel is danced in hard shoes. While this dance has become most popular with audiences around the world who have seen 'Riverdance' and other Irish dance shows, it is rarely (if ever) danced in any competitions. It was this dance with its fast rhythmic beats and spectacular footwork that excited so many millions of people around the world when it was performed on the first 'Riverdance' show for the Eurovision Song Contest. You could say that this turned the Irish dancing world upside down in a few minutes and achieved more publicity and respect for Irish dance than had been achieved in the previous seventy years.

The treble reel style of dance was popularised by The National Folk Theatre (Siamsa Tíre) under the guidance of artistic director Father Pat Ahern and dance teacher Patrica Hanafin from Tralee.

Solo Set Dances

Solo set dances are performed in heavy (hard) shoes to a specific set piece of music or dance tune, and many date back to the middle of the nineteenth century. A set dance tune differs from the ordinary jig or hornpipe in that the last two strictly adhere to an eight-bar structure. The set dance tune usually has two parts, which are referred to by the dancer as 'the step' (first part) and 'the set' (second part); it may not adhere to an eight-bar structure in either the step or the set. In a set dance the dancer is performing to a prescribed tune, so that the footwork and rhythm of the dance are expected to interpret the tune.

The following is a selection of some of the solo set dances:

In 2/4 time – The Blackbird, Downfall of Paris, King of The Fairies, The Lodge Road, Rodney's Glory.

In 6/8 time – The Blackthorn Stick, The Drunken Gauger, The Three Sea Captains, The Orange Rogue, Planxty Drury, Rub The Bag, St Patrick's Day.

In 4/4 time – The Garden of Daises, The Hunt, Kilkenny Races, Madame Bonaparte, The Job of Journeywork, Youghal Harbour.

Ceilis (Irish Group Dances)

Ceili dances are group dances which are performed both in competitions and at ceilis (social dances). These dances, which were around in the nineteenth century in different forms with a variety of steps, were formalised by the Gaelic League at the beginning of the twentieth century. They are all structured on a few basic steps: side step, threes, promenade step, rising step, and rise and grind. If you can master these steps you need only then concentrate on the body and figures of the different dances.

Ceili dances are a collection of dances with a variety of formations – round dances, long line dances and long column dances. Thirty of these are described in books 1, 2, and 3 of the Irish Dance Commission's 'Na Rince Forine', and a complete knowledge of these thirty dances is required when Irish dancers sit their teaching examination. They are danced with very slight local variations throughout the Irish dance world. At ceilis and in competitions dances can differ slightly, the square in the Fairy Reel being a good example. The 4-hand and 8-hand jigs and reels are the most common ceili dances performed in competitions.

From the beginning of the twentieth century ceili dancing was very popular in most parts of Ireland. People travelled great distances to attend a dance and in the largest cities thousands packed the dance halls to participate. An example in Dublin will give a good idea of the situation nationwide. Ceilis were held every Sunday in the Round Room of the Mansion House, Dublin. Each week the hall would be packed to capacity, and often the 'full house' signs were put up before the official starting time.

Apart from Sunday nights in the Mansion House, the Gaelic League had clubs all over Dublin where members could learn dances once or twice a week – these clubs also organised ceilis on Saturday nights. In the late sixties and early seventies there was a decline in numbers, and the regular Sunday night ceilis which were held in the Mansion House were changed to the Clarence Hotel. The smaller dance hall had a great atmosphere after the Round Room of the Mansion which was a beautiful (but vast) room with a very high roof. The quality of the sound in the Clarence Hotel was excellent compared to the unusual acoustics of the Mansion House. In the late seventies the ceilis stopped in the Clarence Hotel and moved to the Na Fianna GAA club on Mobhi Road, Glasnevin, on the north side of Dublin City.

One of the causes of the decline in numbers attending ceili dancing was quite natural given that modern dance had taken off in the late fifties and sixties with the coming of Elvis, The Beatles and all the other pop idols. We had entered a new era of entertainment.

Ceili dances have kept Irish dancing a living social form in Ireland and abroad for more than a hundred years. Apart from the thirty standard dances in books 1, 2 and 3, there are a great many other very popular ceili dances including dances for one, two, three, four, five, six and eight couples. Ceili dances can be danced by children, youth and adults, and for any dancer there is no greater joy than to dance an 8-hand jig or The High Caul Cap with a good group of dancers. Ceili dance classes are mostly held by Irish dance schools but you can also find some ceili clubs which have more emphasis on the social side of ceili dancing as a leisure-time activity.

Social Group Set Dances

These dances, known as 'sets' and 'half sets' in their many localised forms, derive from the quadrille, a dance in which couples faced each other standing in a square. Quadrilles were very popular in the Paris of Napoleon. The victorious armies of Wellington became familiar with them and introduced them to England and Ireland. Dancing masters adapted these dances by substituting native steps for the ballroom steps and by speeding up the time to that of the common reel and jig. Differences developed in the number of figures which ranged from three to six, the usual number being five. The five figures in the original quadrilles required music in 6/8 and 2/4 time.

Social group set dances were almost completely wiped out in the first seventy years of the twentieth century as they were considered foreign by the Gaelic League. Set dances such as the Kerry and Clare sets have come back on the Irish social dance scene in recent years and have proved to be quite popular with the more mature age group.

These dances are not distinctly Irish, as their style and steps can be found in many European countries, especially Russia. Recently, while in Moscow, I was a guest of the Russian Academy of Music and paid a visit to their folk dance archives – there the professor showed me video tapes of dancing which had been collected on field trips in villages and towns throughout Russia. The experts claimed that these dances (quadrilles) had been performed in Russia for more than two hundred years. Later I had the opportunity to see them danced live at the Russian National Festival of Folk Dance in Moscow. The dances I looked at were exactly the same in steps, holds and style as the dances we call sets. I also have seen some very close comparisons in Sweden, Denmark, Latvia, Estonia, Lithuania, Holland, Slovakia, Germany and France. Many of the terms and music rhythms used in set dancing are central European; for example, the mazurka is from Poland, the polka is from the Czech Republic and the waltz is from Austria.

I must say that I am very much in favour of and enjoy all types of dance especially those that give great pleasure to the dancer. I particularly like set dances and can claim to be one of the very small group of people who participated in the revival in Ireland. That was in 1966 in the Clare Man's Club in Bridge Street, Dublin, (near Christ Church Cathedral). Josie and Michael Murphy, a brother and sister from County Clare in the West of Ireland, ran a class teaching the Clare Set, the Caledonian Set, the Plain Set, the Kerry Set and others every Thursday night. To both Josie and Michael should go the credit for the revival of social group set dances – they kept the flame burning and without them I believe set dancing would never have had a revival. They danced and taught the sets because they had a genuine love for them, and at no time did they seek to make profit from their teaching or try to exploit the people who came along to learn from them. They danced the Clare style of dancing, which in my opinion is by far the most graceful, dignified and consistent of all set dance styles. This style makes the performers look like dancers with proper carriage and fine footwork, something which is very rare in most other set dance styles.

The gatherings at the classes in Bridge Street were small – about twenty people each session. Strangely enough, 90 per cent of the attendance were musicians like Sean and James Keane, Michael Tubrity and Mick O'Connor, to name but a few; also the members of the Castle Ceili Band were quite often present to make their contribution. The reason why so few dancers attended the sessions was because set dances were classed as foreign and were forbidden – for any dancer to be caught dancing sets could mean being expelled from an Irish dance class or barred from attending Gaelic League ceilis and events.

There was a small development in social set dancing in the early 1970s, mostly to form teams to enter competitions. At this stage my good friend for many years, the late Connie Ryan, started to take a serious interest in set dancing. Before this I had only seen him dance ceili dances and I had never seen him before in the Clare Man's Club.

It was not until the early 1980s that set dancing started to become known to a wider public. A class given by Joe O'Donovan in 1982 and held at the Willie Clancy Summer School in Milltown Malbay in County Clare was the first introduction to set dancing for most dancers. After this, many social groups developed an interest as set dances were quite easy to dance – the fact that they were very repetitive meant that they could be learnt by almost any beginner. When it became obvious that there was a lot of interest and potential for development amongst the over-forty age group, some individual entrepreneurs became authorities on set dancing overnight. This was one area of dance which was wide open for exploitation. There was nothing written about set dances, there were no rules, no standards, no qualified teachers – it was a free-for-all situation. Teachers could say what they liked and the dancers took it as gospel because very few had the slightest knowledge of dancing and most were new to the Irish dancing scene.

So a new period arrived on the Irish dance scene and full credit must go to my old friend Connie Ryan who could see the great potential for developing social set dancing in a business-like way – with his great organisational ability he set about creating a whole new dance sub-culture in Ireland. He organised busloads of dancers and headed away for weekend set dance courses all over the country. The more weekends were organised the more the need for new dances. At the beginning of this revival there were about half a dozen tried and tested standard set dances including the Kerry Set, the Clare Set, the Plain Set, the Cashel Set and the Caledonian. Today I am sure there are hundreds of them.

Social set dances are often danced at a very fast speed and in a wild manner bearing no resemblance to any of the original set dances, which had a lot of discipline and good manners attached to their character. Before the recent revival, set dancing was never danced in Dublin. Going back to at least before 1860 my father, grandfather and great-grandfather were musicians and dancers, attending dances all over Dublin City and County, and at no time did I ever hear mention of set dancing. When I asked my grandmother, my father and more recently my uncle (who is now 95 and attended dances since he was a child) what they danced, they always said they only performed ceili dances and there were no set dances in their time.

Choreographed Figure Dances

Choreographed figure dances are performed by a team of dancers for a competition or exhibition. This category of dance allows the choreographer the freedom, within limits of style, to create new dances. The patterns of the Book of Kells and other famous manuscripts, or the design of Celtic High Crosses, St Bridget's Cross, Tara brooches and other ancient Irish treasures are all popular themes.

The development of choreographed figure dances in competitions over the last thirty years has produced some very creative and spectacular displays by dance teams, which have added greatly to the entertainment value of Irish dance and have proved to be very popular with dancers, teachers and audiences.

Irish Dancing Today

There is a great demand for solo Irish dancers to perform at all types of events and also the willingness to pay dancers a just and proper reward for their services. Solo dancing is centred around the world of competition. To be really successful and reach a high level most dancers have to attend classes at least twice a week and put in up to four hours' practice every day. The training and dedication required at the highest level of Irish dancing is equal to what is required in any sport, and top Irish dancers can be considered to be excellent athletes.

Ceili dances are exactly the same throughout the Irish dance world, which means ceili dancers worldwide can dance with each other without any problem. In competitions, 4-hand and 8-hand jigs and reels are the most common. Ceili dances can be danced by children, youth and adults – classes are mostly held at Irish dance schools, but you can also find some ceili clubs which have more emphasis on the social side of ceili dancing.

Social group set dances, which are purely social dances, have developed and become popular in Ireland in the last twenty years – they are danced mostly by the more mature age group, the majority of whom would have no previous dance experience. As there is no organisation responsible for set dancing and no standard guidelines or qualified teachers (many people start teaching after only a short period attending classes), it is not possible to give advice on the structures or rules. However, several instruction books have been written recently in a genuine attempt to collect, record and standardise the dances.

I would recommend this form of dance as an excellent leisure-time activity and as the dances are not too difficult one is guaranteed to have fun, lots of laughs and good exercise, while meeting new and old friends. Social set dance evenings are held most weekends in many different venues in Ireland and you may also be lucky to find a session in England, the USA or wherever there may be an Irish community. Although there is no organisation you can contact about classes, most towns in Ireland would have set dance sessions at least once a week. The best way to get information is to ask in the local pub or tourist board, or look on the Internet under 'ceili.com'.

Some benefits of learning Irish dancing are:

Self-Esteem – Increasing poise, personality and confidence.

Increased Mental Skills – Listening, following instructions, increasing attention span, memo rising steps.

Physical Skills – Developing body control and co-ordination.

Friendship – Developing friendships with classmates, fellow performers and ompetitors while taking part in competitions, performances and social events at home and abroad.

Hobby – A very healthy leisure-time activity to occupy dancers in their teens and later years.

Beginners

Irish dance students can start learning as young as 4 years of age but 6 or 7 is more the norm. However, many do not start until their mid-teens.

It is always wise to have a chat with the dance teacher when enrolling in a class and ask the teacher for advice and honest appraisal as to whether your child is ready to join. After one session the teacher would have a very good idea as to whether the time is right for your child. Some 4-year-olds may have no problem in taking dance lessons while others may need to wait until they are just a little older.

Many primary schools have a short course which serves to introduce the children to Irish dance. If children want to progress they must then join an Irish dance school with a qualified teacher affiliated to one of the Irish dance organisations like the Commission for Irish Dance, which is a worldwide organisation, or An Comhdháil, the Irish Dance Teachers' Association, which is based mainly in Dublin but has branches throughout Ireland and also in England and Scotland.

When can a dancer join a class?

Irish dance schools tend to follow an academic calendar, usually the same term as that of the local primary or secondary schools. Most dance teachers use the local school halls. It is normal practice for teachers to accept new students at any time during the year.

How long does an Irish dance class take?

A dance lesson for beginners will take approximately one hour, one afternoon or evening each week. Before special performances or competitions the teacher may call for extra lessons. The student may have to pay extra for these additional classes depending on the circumstances.

Private or semi-private lessons can be arranged with the teacher throughout the year at an agreed schedule.

Do you want your child to dance in competitions or just for pleasure?

Some parents may wish their child to participate in competitions whilst others may only want their child to dance for exercise, pleasure, friendship and cultural reasons.

This need not be a problem but you should make your feelings known to the teacher. Often parents who start with the intention of not allowing their child to take part in competitions change their minds at a later date when the child develops to be a very good dancer. Attending competitions can be a very time-consuming and expensive hobby as you may end up travelling long distances each weekend to participate in the different events.

How long will it take before my child can dance?

It is not possible to say exactly how long this will take. There is no normal progression as it all depends on the dancer's age, talents, commitment and work put in at home outside the class.

When a dancer starts to learn they will begin with the 'threes and sevens' which are the foundation for all Irish dance steps. As time passes you should notice the dancer developing poise and carriage and also improving body alignment.

When learning the 'threes and sevens' they will dance with others performing the same steps in, for example, The Walls of Limerick. This helps the child to develop the all-important sense of timing. In the first months the dancer will also develop hand-holding and other arm movements as well as the execution of steps in dances such as the Siege of Ennis and the Fairy Reel. The teacher will match ages and talents of other dancers when making teams for the 2-, 4-, 6- and 8-hand ceili figure dances.

The next development is to a choreography team which can be a team made up of nine to sixteen dancers. The choreography or exhibition dance demands a lot of hard work and commitment from every member of the team.

As the dancer advances they will be able to execute more complex steps and be able to lift themselves with refinement and grace while dancing. The progression is to move on to hard shoe dances such as hornpipes and treble jigs. The dancer will now need a second kind of shoe ('hard shoes') usually fitted with fibreglass heels and tips (see section on Irish Dancing Shoes). The dancer will now learn to make rhythmic sounds using the toe, heel and ball of the foot. From this stage on you will see the complexity of the steps grow and grow. Soon the dancer will be able to perform set dances (which are danced in hard shoes to a set piece of music) such as King of the Fairies, usually choreographed by the teacher. You will now start to appreciate the special features in solo dancing which are exclusively Irish and not found among the national dances of any other people.

Some teachers include basic ceili dances in their solo class. Others who enter teams for competitions have a separate class for figure and choreographed dances.

After spending some time progressing in the dancing school the dancer can start to be graded. Most organisations have grade examinations, progressing up to the teachers' examination. The examination grades concentrate on basic solo dances and gradually incorporate more advanced steps and ceili dances.

Feiseanna (Competitions)

It is important to note that different Irish dance organisations have different rules and there will be changes in the rules depending on the organisation, region and country. Any Irish dance teacher should be able to advise you as to the rules of a particular place.

The Class Feis

For most dancers this first competition is a small event in which only members of their own dancing school take part. While the class feis is run on the same rules as any other competition, usually it is a fun day and a social occasion for parents and dancers alike. The class feis is usually held before the Christmas or summer breaks.

Grades and Levels

In solo dancing events, dancers compete in one of four levels, depending on their abilities and what awards they have won at previous competitions. Within each of these four levels, competitions are broken down into age groups. The dance competitions are adjudicated by an independent judge who will mark the dancers on Timing (rhythm), Carriage (deportment), Construction of Steps (complexity), and Execution (presentation).

The first of January is the date which decides the age group a dancer will compete in. For example, if the dancer is 14 before the first of January they will dance in the under-15 age group and if they are 14 after the first of January they will dance in the under-14 age group.

There are usually four grades: Beginners (novice), Primary, Intermediate and Open.

Beginners' Competition – This is open to dancers who have never been placed first in a competition for the dance specified. Only basic steps may be danced.

Primary Competition – This is for dancers who have never been placed first for the specific dance in that age group. For example, a dancer who has been placed first for the primary reel under-10s may go on to dance the primary reel under-11s. The steps are still fairly basic but of a higher standard.

Intermediate Competition – This is for competitors who have never been placed first for the specific dance in their age group. Advanced steps are allowed.

Open (or Prizewinners') Competition – This is the highest grade where competitors perform their most intricate steps.

There are competitions for the many individual types of dances, for example, reels, jigs, hornpipes, slip jigs and set dances, but the dancer who participates in a feis can also enter a trophy or championship competition. Primary and intermediate dancers can compete in the trophy competition and open dancers can take part in the championship. Sometimes different competitions have slight variations to the rules so it is always better to get a copy of the syllabus for each different feis which will clearly state the rules.

Almost every weekend you will find an open competition in a region not too far away.

The Open Championship – This level is the most advanced in Irish solo competitions.

The Regional Championships – Each region holds a championship each year, for example, the Ulster, Munster, Leinster and Connacht Championships.
You will also have the same regional championships in England, the USA, Canada, Australia and other countries. The dancers must dance one soft shoe and one hard shoe dance plus one or two set dances according to their age group. Approximately one in ten competitors from the Regional Championships qualify for the World Championships. There are three adjudicators.

The National Championships – At this level you have the All Ireland, the All England, the North America, All Australia and the All Canada Championships. There are three or five adjudicators.

The World Championship – It is almost every competitive dancer's aim to dance in the World Irish Dancing Championship. To dance in the very top competition, dancers have to qualify by competing in regional and national championships.

The World Irish Dancing Championships are usually held over the Easter holidays each year in Ireland but will be hosted outside Ireland for the first time in the year 2002 in the Clyde Auditorium, Glasgow, Scotland.
Dancers dance a soft and hard shoe dance plus one or two set dances according to the age group. There are five or seven adjudicators.

Changing Dancing Schools

There are certain rules to be abided by when a dancer wants to change their class and these differ from one organisation to another. The teacher will be able to advise what the rules are in an organisation – for example, the rule was (and may still be) that if dancers change schools they have to serve a period of six months when they are not allowed to dance in open competitions. This is today called a 'restyling period'.

The reason for such rules having to be applied is that teachers can give a great amount of time and effort training dancers, bringing them from beginners to a very advanced stage. At this stage of their development – if they are of high standard – it is not unusual for some teachers to poach dancers from another school, which is a very unfair practice when one considers the time spent cultivating and grooming young dancers.

There are several reasons why a dancer may want to change dancing schools:

When they have to move out of the district where their school is located.

When there are no dancers of their age group in their class.

When relationships between the teacher or fellow dancers in the class become unpleasant.

When other schools participate in more public performances, exhibitions, shows and attractive trips abroad to international festivals.

Changing Organisations

The most common reason for dancing schools changing organisations is that the standard of dancing is much higher amongst the general membership of the organisation they are members of – this means that schools which are of a lower standard have very little hope of ever winning competitions against the better dancers. If the dancers do not win any medals, most will eventually give up. Therefore the teacher often changes to an organisation which has a standard equal to the level of their dancing school.

Some organisations give every dancer who enters a competition a medal. It is a great pity that a large number dance only to compete and win medals, rather than for the love of dancing. Usually it is the parents and not the teachers who are the biggest medal-hunters, as they take their children travelling to competitions all over the country weekend after weekend in search of prizes.

Entering competitions is, however, very good in moderation because it gives the dancers something to aim for, and tends to lead to a much greater work rate, which in turn leads to a higher standard of dancing.

Becoming a Teacher

The next step on the road for many dancers who have achieved all they set out to do is to become a teacher. To sit the TCRG Teachers' Examination you need to be at least 20 years old. The exams are held every year in several different locations – normally there are two exams held in Dublin, and one each in the USA, Australia and the United Kingdom.

The exam is divided into four sections: teaching, theory, music and dancing. The teaching section examines both ceili and solo teaching with a practical exam involving a real lesson. The theory section, which is considered by most to be the most difficult part, is a two-hour written test on the thirty ceili dances from the Irish Dance Commission's books 1, 2 and 3. The written music test examines the candidate's knowledge of all the music necessary to accompany dances. It is also necessary to identify tunes, timing, bars etc. – thirteen set dance tunes are played and you must be able to recognise at least nine. The dancing section requires that the candidate can dance to a good standard. They are asked to perform light and heavy dances along with three set dances from a list of six which are nominated by the candidate (three in hornpipe time and three in jig time) plus two of the nominated traditional set dances. Dancers sitting the exam who plan to teach in Ireland also have to do a test in the Irish language as they are expected to be able to teach through this medium.

If a candidate fails a section of the exam, they do not have to repeat the whole exam again, only the section which was failed. If you fail three times in a row you must repeat the whole exam.

The above applies to dancers sitting the exams with the Irish Dance Commission – with An Coimisiún you sit all the exam at one time, while An Comhdháil dancers take two sections one year and the second two the following year.

Becoming an Adjudicator

Next step in the ladder after becoming a teacher is to become an adjudicator. First requirement is that you are at least 30 years old and hold your TCRG. The content of the examination is very much the same as the teachers' exam, as well as being tested in adjudication at a small feis for the day and then being interviewed about decisions and results. Again the rule applies for any person who resides in Ireland or intends to teach there – they must take an oral Irish examination.

Becoming an Examiner

To become an examiner you need to have been an adjudicator for at least ten years. This position of examiner used to be handed down but recently An Coimisiún have set exams for the position.

Irish Dancing Costumes

Up to this century there is very little evidence of a distinctive Irish dancing costume because Ireland was so long under the influence of British rule, especially from the seventeenth to the nineteenth centuries. There is almost no reference to the clothes worn by dancers in early literature, and those descriptions that are given suggest that the dancers wore ordinary clothes of the period. Dinely (1681) refers to dancers wearing their 'holiday apparel', or Sunday best as we might say today. Kennedy, in his book The Banks of the Boro, gave the following description of the dress worn by dancers performing the Rince Fada in 1812: 'They were in their shirtsleeves, waistcoats, knee breeches, white stockings and turn-pumps. The girls were in their Sunday garb with their hair decked with ribbons.' O'Rafferty and O'Rafferty (1953) illustrate what a group of dancers in the eighteenth century probably looked like: 'The girls wearing shoulder shawls held at the waist by red-laced belts and long skirts, often tucked up to the waist to facilitate the dancing, the men wearing short coats, knee breeches, stockings and a high-low hat.' Since this was typical eighteenth-century dress it was almost certainly worn by the dancers of that period.

In the Pearse Museum, Rathfarnham, there are photographs from the end of the nineteenth century which show Irish dancers at a festival in Wexford. The boys are wearing waistcoats, collars and ties, long-sleeved shirts, knee breeches and long socks. The girls are wearing pretty full-length dresses with long sleeves, white collars and cuffs; the dresses are very full and look exactly like those they would have worn for Sunday best.

The foundation of the Gaelic League in 1893 led to a great Gaelic cultural revival in Ireland and also to the beginning of the Irish dance costume as we know it today. The League resolved to create a costume or form of dress for all those associated with the Gaelic revival – this dress had to be distinctively Irish.

Male Costumes

Knee Breeches

Before the kilt was introduced, knee breeches were very popular with Irish male dancers – there are a great many photographs available showing them being worn from the late nineteenth century.

These were imported from England in the eighteenth century and were used by some dancers up to the 1920s and 1930s when it became necessary to wear kilts in Irish dancing competitions if you were to have any chance of success.

The Kilt

The start of the twentieth century saw the introduction of the kilt as part of the accepted dress for those involved in the Gaelic movement. We must take into consideration the period and feelings at the time – there was a great need to express Irish national identity and distinguish the Irish dress, and the introduction of the kilt as part of the Irish costume was seen as helping to fulfil this need.

The kilt was in daily use by members of the Gaelic League and its supporters. For example, it was very much part of the school uniform for the students of Patrick Pearse's college (St Enda's) in 1908, and they would have worn the kilt while learning and performing Irish dancing, which was part of their curriculum. Patrick Pearse organised a great many open-air festivals of music, song and dance in the beautiful grounds of St Enda's Estate, Rathfarnham, where this college moved to in 1910. Several of the original programmes for these open-air festivals still exist in the Pearse Museum, and exhibitions of Irish dances, such as the 4-hand and 8-hand reels and solo dances, are quite clearly listed.

There is said to be a photograph of Peader O'Rafferty after winning the First Ulster Irish Dance Championship in 1911 and in it Peader is wearing a kilt. It is possible that this is the earliest record of a competitive dancer wearing one.

The kilt was not formalised as part of an Irish dancing school until probably the early 1920s when Lily Comerford, the well-known Irish dance teacher from Dublin, introduced it as part of her dancing school costume.

The Tailteann Games in Dublin in 1924 was an occasion when dancers came from all over Ireland to perform. It was also the first time that many dancers from country regions saw the kilt being used as part of an Irish dancing school uniform. By the 1930s the use of the kilt by male dancers had spread to all parts of Ireland.

Up to the 1960s the most popular colour for the kilts was saffron and green. This developed to a much greater selection of colours, including red and black, which were used with matching ties and shawls. The Irish dancing kilt was usually judged by the quality of material and the number of pleats. My own kilt, which I still have in a wardrobe somewhere, had thirty-two pleats – one for each county of Ireland.

For a period of over seventy years it was, as everybody believed, compulsory for males to wear a kilt in Irish dancing competitions – not to wear one was unknown because if you didn't, you had no hope of ever winning. Then along came 'Riverdance' in April 1994 with its costume of black trousers – immediately after, these became the accepted costume for competitions. Because of the overwhelming support throughout the world for 'Riverdance' and also because most male Irish dancers wanted to move with this new fashion, the organisation responsible for making and implementing the rules of Irish dancing for almost seventy years announced that there never really was a rule that boys must wear kilts! What a pity this information could not have been made known many years ago, as it is certain that having to wear a kilt was responsible for putting the majority of boys off learning Irish dancing.

Aran Sweaters

The wearing of the heavy Aran knitted sweater, along with a knitted cap and Aran crios, was popular for a short time in the 1950s and 1960s, but more for team and ceili dancing. This costume was traditional and was made popular by the Clancy Brothers ballad group.

The hand-knitted Aran sweaters were much too warm to dance in and were best suited for their original purpose – keeping the Aran Islanders warm, especially when fishing. Each family on the Aran Islands had its own distinctive pattern for its sweaters. The reason for this is said to be when fishermen were lost at sea and not found for some time, the only means of identifying the body was the remains of the Aran sweater and its pattern.

Costumes Today

The male dancers since the 1920s have been wearing a jacket which could have been used in everyday dress. In the early years the jacket was usually of Irish tweed but in recent years a great variety of colours and materials have been used. Today most dancers wear a very smart outfit with matching colours for the socks, tie or the kilt, with a toning or contrasting jacket.

Since the 'Riverdance' show many male dancers have taken to wearing black trousers and blouse-type shirts which is a very healthy development for male Irish dancers.

Female Costumes

In many European countries the baron responsible for the village or region would once a year present his workers and their families with a length of cloth to make a new costume for wearing on Sundays and special occasions. The length of cloth was usually the same colour, which meant that all the women from the village would have the same costume. The people from neighbouring villages would have been given a different colour, so it was easy to tell which village a person came from by the colour of their costume. This tradition is still practised today in some villages in Germany, Austria and South Tyrol.

People in Ireland were not so fortunate as to have landlords or squires who carried out this tradition. They were lucky if they were allowed to keep a roof over their head. Life for the Irish peasant was very difficult and clothes were simple and functional. The climate was damp, and men and women wore woollen cloaks known as 'brats'. These garments had an attached hood to be pulled over the head on a cold day, and the cloak would be fastened to the shoulder by a Tara brooch, or tied under the chin with a black bow or corded ribbon.

These cloaks were worn all over Ireland in the seventeenth century by rich and poor alike. Examples of names given to the cloaks were the Kinsale Cloak and the Bandon Cloak, because they were worn in these County Cork towns up until very recent times. The wool was particularly thick and durable, being resistant to the weather. Black, red, blue and grey were the most popular colours – red was particularly found in many parts of the country, as the madder root was used as a dye. (The madder was a herbaceous plant with yellowish flowers and a red dye was obtained from the root.) A mother would present her daughter with a new cloak on her wedding day and this would be kept for special occasions, the old one being worn for going to market.

Female dancers wore these quite heavy cloaks and hoods with long dresses as a dancing costume in the nineteenth century. One can only imagine that they must have been severely restricted in their movement and in the length of time they could dance because of the weight and heat of the costume. The traditional cloak worn by female dancers up to the beginning of this century has been adapted to a half-drape – it has an embroidered Celtic design and is worn for decoration only.

Following the Gaelic Revival in the beginning of this century, women took to wearing a special type of dress. This was very often of white 'bawneen' with green ribbons and was worn on Sundays and special occasions. In the 1920s and 1930s came the introduction of what was to become the recognised dancing class costume for the women: a pleated dress, with a coatee worn over this, and a shawl of the same colour as the dress, sually attached at one shoulder, and either hanging straight down the back or else draped over and caught up onto the opposite hip. Wearing of the coatee was very fashionable from the 1930s onwards but, like the pleated dress, became very rare in the 1980s with the tendency for a full-sleeved dress with a more flared effect to the lower half. While some of the dresses worn today may contain a single or small number of pleats, the accordion-type pleated dress is seen rarely.

Embroidery

Man first carved patterns on stone, metal, wood and pottery, and then later came embroidery. With the development of materials, patterns were put on clothes. Superstition and belief in the power of evil led to cosmic symbols being used wherever there was an opening in the garment. Embroidery was used around the neck and openings in shirts and blouses – cuffs, edges of sleeves and hems. These were all protected with decorative symbols. Throughout the years these symbols became embellished with many decorative patterns. Many of the designs changed completely – the circle became a sun, wheel or flower, the spiral became a serpent, triangles became stars and the tree of life carried many motifs.

Stitchcraft became very important – there was a significance in whether the stitches passed from left to right or east to west. The cross, used both in stitching and design, represented the four cardinal points of the world with a fifth point being in a vertical direction arising from the centre. Known as the cosmic quadrangle, it was an important symbol of life. Every country developed its own individual designs and within a country each region, village and valley had variations.

In the 1920s Irish dance costumes started to display a limited amount of coloured thread embroidery. Over the years the amount of embroidery has increased to alarming proportions. The art of hand-machined and computer-designed embroidery has reached magnificent heights in many of the dance costumes being worn today. This is said to be Celtic embroidery, since most of the designs are said to be based on Celtic ornamentation from the Book of Kells. Nowadays some of the designs have become very modern with the introduction of silver and gold threads and the use of glitter (rhinestones) and glittering sequins, and would appear to have no traditional or Celtic meaning.

Crochet Collars and Cuffs

A most pleasant development in the ladies' costume was the beautiful, elaborate and intricate crochet collars and cuffs, sometimes made of wool-like material but more often of lace. In recent years the colours of these collars and cuffs (with matching hairbands or rosettes) has changed from being white to almost any colour.

Stockings

Long black stockings were previously worn by the older female dancers, with the younger girls wearing short white ankle socks. Since the 1980s there has been a change to almost all female dancers wearing white calf-length socks which are often referred to as poodle socks.

Colours

The colours used in the ladies' dresses in the period following the Gaelic League foundation were mostly white or green. The colour red was avoided due to its being looked upon as English. This was regrettable, since red was the most popular colour in skirts and petticoats worn by the Irish women up to the middle of the last century.

More recently the number of colours in use in both male and female costumes has increased enormously so that every shade is now in evidence. Dark navy and black velvet appeared to be most popular in the 1980s, one of the reasons being that these dark colours showed off the embroidery at its best. In the 1990s we have seen the introduction of bright luminous colours with hair bands, costume lining and underwear all matching – the use of these colours means that the present female Irish dance costume has gone as far away from the traditional colours as one can go.

Hair

Hair style is considered by dancers to be one of the most important parts of preparation for a feis and the image of Irish dancers with a headful of tight ringlets is a common one. The trend today is for dancers of all ages to wear wigs. This saves many hours of work putting in the different rollers, curlers and rags for often twenty-four hours before a competition and needing great patience by all concerned. The wigs are also very convenient for those with short or very straight hair.

Costumes Today

Today each dancing class or school has its own distinctive costume. Solo dancers have their own individually designed – most possess both a class costume and a solo costume (or two or three). Since the coming of 'Riverdance' there have been a few changes. Some dancing classes and solo dancers have made a complete change in the style of their dress. Instead of a very expensive elaborately embroidered costume, many dancers are wearing a very simply designed dress in plain colours and with very little decoration around the sleeves and neck. The dress is short and black tights are normally worn. This costume is only an extra in the wardrobe of the Irish dancer, more keeping in fashion with the 'Riverdancers', but it will hardly replace the very elaborate and colourful Irish dance costume which has taken almost seventy-five years to develop.

The cost of the Irish dance costume has always been very expensive and today it has greatly increased, so much so that some dancers have to retire from competition dancing as they cannot afford to keep up with the latest fashion. The production of costumes and supply of dancing costume accessories is now a big business in itself, small factories and shops having been set up to meet these needs, not only in Ireland but also abroad.

Irish Dancing Shoes

In comparison with other items of clothing, shoes have changed very little over the years. In social circles shoes went through every conceivable style and shape, although the changes did not affect the rural workers, who were not encouraged to emulate their masters. For the land, a tough and long-lasting shoe was essential and peasants found a simple design that was economical and practical. Shoes were an expensive status symbol and were not easily made in the home because the work required the instruments of the shoe-maker's craft. Early settlers wore no shoes and it was not unusual to find country people walking for miles barefoot and putting on their shoes just before entering town.

One of the earliest forms of shoe or sandal was probably made from woven palm leaves, papyrus or vegetable fibre. The design was very simple and the shoe was kept in place by bands of linen or leather thongs. Various names were given to the early form of shoe, one being the Latin 'solea' from which comes the English word 'sole'.

Irish dance shoes today are made from hard or soft durable leather according to the type of dance being performed. The man's shoes for light dances are of a plain design with soft leather uppers and thin leather soles. The ladies wear dancing pumps for light dances such as the slip jig and reel. Jig shoes, which are used for what are called heavy dances, have plain leather uppers and leather soles with built-up toe pieces, so that the dancer can get greater sound from their beats. Up to some years ago these toe pieces were made from several layers of leather which were tapered at the back. Some dancers liked to have a large number of nails hammered into the toe piece to assist with the sound. Today there are very strict rules regarding nails that can be used in dancers' shoes in competitions – any form of metal on the soles or heels is not allowed. Metal taps, such as those used by tap dancers, have never been allowed in Irish dance competitions because this would mean that their beats were artificially assisted and therefore not recognised as pure beats.

In recent years the biggest breakthrough in the development and improvement of materials for dancing shoes has been fibreglass. This has become the most popular material for the heels and toe pieces because it is very much lighter and gives much better wear than leather. It also produces a better sound quality. The only problem is that sometimes the fibreglass heels tend to crack or a piece of the heel breaks away.

One of the latest additions to the development of Irish dancing shoes is the bubble heel which is often hollow and made from plastic. The advantage of the bubble heel is that it allows dancers to perform the clicks much easier as the sides of the heel extend out in a bubble-like shape. Very definite clicking sounds are made in the movement when a dancer leaps into the air and clicks one heel against the other. (Performing clicks are a very important part of Irish dancing and if a dancer misses a click in a competition it can mean a loss of important points.) Bubble heels have not been accepted by some organisations and are not allowed in dance competitions, possibly because it is felt that they lessen the skill of performing the clicks and therefore give the dancers wearing bubble heels an unfair advantage.

The very latest development in Irish dancing shoes is what is called the flexie sole. The flexie sole has had the spine removed from the sole and this gives the shoe much greater flexibility. However, this latest development has not been fully tested and is still under review, as it is not yet known what effect the flexie sole might have on the dancer's feet.

The use of fibreglass, plastic heels, flexie soles and bubble heels have all contributed to the changing styles and trends that have kept Irish dancing more alive and exciting than ever.

In stage shows such as 'Lord of the Dance' and 'Riverdance' you can quite clearly see the metal heels, toe pieces and taps which are worn by some of the principal dancers for special effects and sounds. These would not be accepted for competition or other purposes, as they would be considered to create an artificially assisted sound and are quite clearly tap-dance shoes. Modern technology also allows for radio microphones to be placed in the toe piece of the shoes which produces greater amplification of the sound and rhythm.

Cultural Organisations and Dance In Ireland

The Irish Dance Commission

As there were a great many irregularities in competitions which often led to fierce disputes, Irish dance teachers found there was a need to look at the organisation and co-ordination of schools, teachers and competitions. In 1929 the Gaelic League established an enquiry into the state of Irish dancing, known as the Dance Commission – as a result, recommendations were made as to how the problems could be rectified. In 1931 the Dance Commission reported back to the Gaelic League General Meeting and made recommendations that a body should be set up to do everything necessary to promote Irish dancing (both ceili and step dancing) and exercise control of all persons connected with it – adjudicators, teachers, dancers and organisers of competitions. The proposals were accepted and the body who made the recommendations – the Irish Dance Commission – were considered best suited to take on the work of implementing the proposals.

The Commission was composed as follows: six elected by the Executive Council of the Gaelic League, three each elected by the Councils of the Gaelic League in each province, three elected by the Dublin Irish Dance Teachers' Association and three elected by the Irish Music Society. The make-up of the Commission was very important for the future of Irish dance and, when you see that of the twenty-four members only three needed to be from an Irish dancing association, the balance was more in favour of Irish speakers than dancers. In later years this unbalanced representation of dance teachers, practitioners and experts was unfortunately to lead to several disagreements over policy and in 1969 ended in a great division in Irish dancing which was most regrettable. A large number of well-known dancing teachers decided to terminate their relationships with the Commission and continued organising Irish dance through their own organisation, called An Comhdháil na Muinteoirí Rincí Gaelacha (The Irish Dance Teachers' Association). This unfortunate division in Irish dancing meant that some of the most famous teachers left the Commission, people like Harry McCaffrey, Cora Cadwell, Rory O'Connor, Maggie Kane, Peggy McTeggart, Cormac O'Keeffe, Anna McCoy, and Peter Bolton to name a few.

While there were many questionable rules brought in by the Dance Commission, the one considered to be most offensive and destructive to the development of Irish dance was 'the Ban' which forbade any member dancer or teacher to participate or assist in any dancing other than Irish. In other words, the individual was denied the freedom of creative expression and not allowed to have an interest in other forms of dance, as well as folk cultures of other lands. Another rule was that dancers were not allowed to enter competitions unless all items worn were manufactured in Ireland.

Up to 1950 most of the Irish Dance Commission's activities were confined to Ireland – since then it has spread to many countries around the world and today has more than 1,500 qualified teachers worldwide.

The Irish Dance Teachers' Association

Known as 'An Comhdháil', the Irish Dance Teachers' Association pre-dated the Irish Dance Commission. Associations existed in most large cities and towns in Ireland in the early 1920s and (further afield) even as far away as Melbourne, Australia.

When in 1929 the Gaelic League set up a commission of inquiry into the running of Irish dancing rules and regulations for competitions, several members of the Teachers' Association were invited onto this. When a permanent commission was set up, three members of the Association became members, namely Tom Lawlor, Dinney Cuffe and Mrs Lynch.

On its foundation, the Irish Dance Commission accepted the qualifications of the members of the Teachers' Association. Until 1941, when the Commission started its own examinations for teachers and adjudicators, the only possible way to become an officially recognised dance teacher was with the Irish Dance Teachers' Association. Some of the most famous teachers received their qualification certification this way, including Cormac O'Keeffe, Tom Lawlor, Maggie Kane, Essie Connolly and Mae Butler.

The Teachers' Association continued to hold meetings, attended by most teachers and Commission members, and recommendations passed at annual conventions were conveyed to the Commission for implementation. Dissatisfaction over Irish dancing came to a climax in 1969–70 with teachers having to affiliate with either organisation. The Irish Dance Teachers' Association terminated its affiliation with the Commission and became an independent organisation with its own revised constitution. It developed its own membership throughout Ireland, England and Scotland, holding its own examinations for teachers and adjudicators as well as running regional and national championships.

Comhaltas Ceoltóirí Éireann

This was founded in March 1951 when a group of Irish traditional musicians, which included the master piper Leo Rowsome, met to discuss the holding of a traditional music festival in Mullingar, County Westmeath. The festival of music was organised for June of the same year. This was the beginning of the Fleadh Cheoil na hÉireann. At first the festival was a small affair, mainly competitions and a few sessions in the local pubs, but after several years the numbers attending went from hundreds to thousands and today it is one of the premier traditional music festivals to be found in Europe.

The main aims of the organisation are the preservation of the harp, the uilleann pipes and Irish traditional music. The development of Comhaltas was steady – it developed branches all over Ireland and then started to mushroom all over the world. In the mid-sixties there were two branches in Dublin: The Pipers' Club, which held sessions in a small room in Thomas Street on Saturday nights, and the Clontarf Branch, which held sessions in the North Star Hotel on Friday nights. These sessions were strictly music sessions and only on the odd occasion did you have the opportunity to dance. The policy was that the musicians were there to learn new tunes and to enjoy each other's music – it would be hard to disagree with their view. There were many fine musicians who attended, including Leo Rowsome and his family, Seamus Ennis, Tom Glacken and his family, Vincent Crehan and his family, the two great gentlemen of Irish music, Frank Higgins and John Joe Gardiner, and the grand old lady of Irish music, Mrs Kathleen Harrington. There were also many young musicians of the future including Sean Keane, James Keane, Paddy Glacken, John Regan, Liam Ó Floinn, Tony Smith, Brian and Pat O'Kane, Helena Rowsome, Mick Allen and a dashing young dancer, Donncha Ó Muineachain. For almost seven years I seldom missed a music session with the Clontarf branch because of the good music and friendly atmosphere. The same could be said, I am sure, for all the Comhaltas branches and its members.

In 1969 and 1970 some dance development started. On 27–28 November 1969 the first Scoraiocht (cabaret) producers' course was held in Birr. The director of the course was Father Pat Ahern who was Artistic Director of Siamsa Tíre, the National Folk Theatre, and a very talented musician and producer. A group of us were invited to dance and assist with production.

The first Comhaltas Scoraiocht (Cabaret Show), held in Colaiste Mhuire, Parnell Square, Dublin on 21 December 1969, had a dance team which was part of the show including Donncha Ó Muineachain, Connie Ryan, Sean Kennedy and myself. We danced ceili dances or dances specially arranged by Donncha Ó Muineachain with ceili dance steps.

In the March/April 1970 edition of Treoir, the Comhaltas magazine, Donncha Ó Muineachain who was the driving force for the development of dance in Comhaltas, wrote an article encouraging Comhaltas committees to start developing a ceili dance class and even solo dancing so that Comhaltas could enter a new field of Irish culture – this would represent a major expansion and step forward for this go-ahead organisation. The first ceili dance instructors' course was held in Birr on 11–12 April 1970.

The first Fleadh Nua (New Festival) was held on the 30 May–1 June 1970 in Croke Park. We danced ceili dances and arrangements with ceili dance steps. Father Pat Aherne was the producer/director of the event.

In 1970 we danced at a great many Comhaltas events, such as the Fleadh Cheoil, concerts and cabarets. I was also present at the first Tionol Cheoil Seisiun (musical gathering) which was held in Franciscans College, Gormanstown, County Meath. The purpose of organising all these events was the promotion and preservation of music and song.

There were always great dances at the Fleadh Cheoil na hÉireann every year. These were wild and hectic evenings when approximately 80 per cent of the attendance knew nothing about Irish dance and were mostly inspired by Guinness or good Irish whiskey. This was an occasion when the regular Irish dancers had to take a back seat, but sure, everybody enjoyed themselves and that's what it was all about.

It was in the early seventies before Comhaltas Ceoltóirí Éireann started to take a serious interest in dance. One of the reasons for this development was the fact that the Dance Commission had split, so organisations such as RTÉ (the Irish national television station) had problems getting dancers for their Irish entertainment programmes. For example, if they used members of one organisation, the other organisation would make a strong protest. RTÉ did not want to be involved in the dispute so they looked elsewhere. Sadly this led to the end of the very popular weekly television show called 'Club Ceili' which was an hour-long programme dedicated to Irish dance, music and song, and had a team of about thirty performing all types of Irish dancing. Unfortunately for Irish dance, 'Club Ceili' was never repeated nor to this day has there been a television Irish dance programme to equal it.

The conflict in the Irish dance organisations led to the beginning of Comhaltas Ceoltóirí Éireann's strong input into Irish television – since dancers were a very important requirement for any Irish television programme, dancing developed within the organisation. As Comhaltas wanted to be independent from the Irish dancing organisations which were having political problems, they put a strong emphasis on group set dancing, which was banned by the Irish Dance Commission because it was claimed to be foreign dance and was just about starting to develop at that time. As there were no rules, regulations, standards or qualifications laid down for set dancing, any person could teach and become an overnight authority on the subject. In April 1976 Comhaltas Ceoltóirí Éireann moved to its own permanent home and headquarters – 'The Culturlann' in Belgrave Square, Monkstown, County Dublin. This was to help with the promotion of dancing as there was a very fine hall in the building. Great credit must go to Tomas Mac Eoin and Donncha Ó Muineachain for their great work and commitment to the development of Irish dance in Comhaltas, and to Billy Boylan who has been running the dances in most recent years.

Comhaltas Ceoltóirí Éireann have done a remarkable job worldwide at developing and preserving Irish traditional music. Today hundreds of branches exist throughout the world and I am happy to say I still have many friends in the organisation going back to those early days.

The Gaelic Athletic Association

The GAA is an amateur Irish sports organisation – most of its teams have social clubs with licensed bars which are often the centre of the cultural life in the club.

Its main input into the development of Irish dance is in the form of weekly ceilis which are run as fundraising and social events in their clubs. Most of the participants would be club members who after having a few social drinks join in the dancing.

In the early 1970s the association started to organise competitions amongst its member clubs to create an interest in other aspects of Irish culture (such as Irish music, dance and song) in the off-season when there was no football or other games. They called the competition 'Scor' which means large gathering. While the cultural competitions were successful and developed into a popular annual event they did not have any real impact on the standard or development of Irish dance.

Gael Linn

Gael Linn is an organisation which promotes and markets Irish cultural events, music recordings, audio tapes, CDs, videos and books. Gael Linn also runs many educational projects such as Irish language classes.

In 1969 Gael Linn decided to organise a nationwide competition for schools – this involved teams performing Irish music, song, dance and drama. The first year's final was held in Dublin with 1,500 young people taking part and this figure has risen to over 50,000 in recent years. The competition, which demands great organisation and funding, is well worth the effort as it gives a great opportunity to many talented young people at a very early age and has started many on the road to successful careers in the music world.

The Irish National Folk Dance Company

The Irish National Folk Dance Company was founded in 1970. Its main aim is to promote Irish and international dance and culture at home and abroad – this is achieved by strengthening ties with other communities and fostering a deeper understanding of Irish heritage. Since its foundation, the company has made over 160 international tours, representing Ireland in twenty-two countries. This involved the training of over 3,000 dancers from all over Ireland and abroad. The company is a non-profit-making arts and cultural organisation.

Apart from organising solo, ceili and set dancing courses, the company aims to develop an understanding of the cultures of other lands. Its archives and library contain folk music and dance material from more than fifty countries. The company motto is 'Music has no Borders'.

The Irish National Folk Dance Company provides a great variety of classes, workshops and seminars on Irish dance. Since 1971 over 8,000 enthusiasts from all over the world come to attend these courses which are combined with a good cultural social programme. The company also specialises in running workshops abroad and to date has organised dance classes in more than twenty-three countries. All the dance company teachers are qualified, very experienced and are representative of the different Irish dance styles and organisations.

Since 1991 the company has had its headquarters in St Enda's, which is the college founded by Patrick Pearse, the great Irish cultural educationist and leader of the 1916 Easter Rising. St Enda's, a very important national monument and special shrine to Irish people all over the world, is located in Rathfarnham, at the foot of the Dublin Mountains and a short journey south of the city centre. Set in fifty acres of beautiful gardens, parkland, rivers and walks, it is also the venue for numerous concerts and cultural events.

St Enda's National Historic Park is well worth a visit. Buses 16 and 16C run from the city centre and the journey takes twenty to thirty minutes.

The Irish Folklore Department in University College Dublin

The Irish Folklore Department in UCD has a magnificent archive of folklore material which has been collected from all over Ireland. The library is said to be one of the best in the world and includes written accounts of folklore, audio, film and video recordings. It is possible to visit the department if you are in Dublin but you should telephone first to make an appointment.

The Irish Traditional Music Archives

The Irish Traditional Music Archives is totally funded by the State and has the largest library of traditional music, song and dance in Ireland. It contains the vast collection of Breandán Breathnach (who died in 1985) and was set up by the Irish Government in response to the need to find a home for this collection. The archives, with the help of modern equipment and computers, provide a very efficient service to make the material available to researchers and interested members of the public.

The Irish Traditional Music Archives is situated at 63 Merrion Square, a very central location on the south side of Dublin City and a fifteen-minute walk from O'Connell Bridge.

'Ceol' – The Irish Traditional Music, Song and Dance Interpretative Centre

In 1999 a new and exciting centre for researchers, enthusiasts and lovers of Irish music, song and dance was opened in the Smithfield Market area of Dublin's north city. This centre is a private initiative by an Irish-American family and has received no state funding. The complex includes a hotel, recording studio, concert hall, large multimedia interpretative centre and a number of traditional music shops. It was named in honour of Chicago police chief Captain O'Neill, perhaps the greatest collector and publisher of Irish music, who up to then had never received the true recognition he deserved in Ireland.

The development shows what can be done when professional people with creative thinking and good vision take on the task of showing and promoting Irish traditional culture. Unequalled in Ireland, the centre is an excellent place to visit for lovers of Irish music and dance as it gives the complete story of Irish folk culture and allows you, with the aid of modern audio-visual technology, to be right in the centre of the dancing.

A visit to the centre is a must when you visit Dublin. It is well situated near the Four Courts (along the north side of the River Liffey), about twelve minutes from O'Connell Bridge.

Music in Ireland

Ireland shows its respect for its ancient music by being one of the few countries in the world to have an instrument, the harp, as its national emblem, appearing on government documents, coins and flags.

Irish music roots go back a long way and in this chapter I will give a short background so you can have an idea of how old the Irish music tradition is and the great influence it had on Europe and other parts of the world.

Origins

Music is said to have been first brought to Ireland by the Tuatha De Danann in approximately 1600 BC. The first reference to music in Ireland was made by the great geographer, Hecataeus of Miletus. Quoted by Diodorus, he describes the Celts of Ireland (c. 500 BC) as singing songs in praise of Apollo and playing melodiously on the harp.

In his book History of Irish Music (1904), Grattan Flood wrote: 'In ancient Ireland the systems of law and medicine were set to music, being poetical compositions.' This quote negates the common misconception that writing did not exist before St Patrick – he certainly introduced a form of Roman script but there existed before him an ancient Celtic alphabet based on Ogham. This was called 'Bethluisnin' or Birch Alder tree and is derivable from a tree or branch. These Irish letters (sixteen in number, although looking in a dictionary today it says there were twenty) were unique in their kind – interestingly, the trees were called after the letters and not the letters after the trees as some have alleged. The Ogham inscriptions, which have survived the hurly-burly of seventeen centuries, are mostly of stone, though they were also written on rings, wooden tablets, ivory, bone, gold, silver, lead, crystals, twigs, etc. While some of them are decidedly Christian, the greater number are pagan.

Music pupils in pre-Christian Irish schools would have been equipped with music staves. These were squared staves which were used for walking or defence when closed and, when open in the shape of a fan, for writing on. Flood quotes Constantine Nigra: 'The first certain examples of rhyme are found in Celtic soil and amongst Celtic nations, in songs made by poets.'

It is important to note that the Irish of the sixth century had knowledge of scale, harmony and counter-point, whilst the plain songs of Rome were very elementary. Irish monks, who were very skilled music masters, travelled all over Europe teaching and setting up music schools and monasteries. One example was the world-renowned monastery of St Gall in Switzerland. It was founded in the year AD 612 by St Gall (or Gallus), whose name has been Latinized from Cellach. This great Irishman, a student of Bangor, County Down, and friend and disciple of St Columbanus, died on 16 October 646. The fame of his music school became known far and near.

In the late seventh and early eighth centuries, Irish music masters had a very strong influence on European music. Kessel, a learned historian, said of the Irish monks:

Every province in Germany proclaims this race as its benefactor. Austria celebrates St Colman, St Virgilius, St Modestus and others. To whom but the ancient Irish was due the famous 'Schattenkloister of Vienna?' Salzburg, Ratisbon, and all of Bavaria honour St Virgilius as their apostle … The Saxons and the tribes of Northern Germany are indebted to them to an extent which may be judged by the fact that the first ten bishops belonged to that race.

So we see that from a very early age Irish music was healthy and strong. To find out how today's dance music was preserved and developed we must look at the great composers and music collectors of the nineteenth and early twentieth centuries like Bunting, Petrie, Pigot, Joyce, O'Farrell, Hudson, and Francis O'Neill. As far as dance music is concerned, the most colourful was O'Neill, who ended his career as Chief Superintendent of Police in Chicago. Due to their work and the Society for the Preservation and Publication of The Melodies of Ireland, which was founded in 1851, Ireland inherited a rich legacy of dance music.

A conservative estimate puts the figure at over 6,000 individual pieces – reels, hornpipes, jigs, and hundreds of tunes for polkas, slides, marches, waltzes and many other dances.

Irish Music Instruments

Ancient Instruments

In the National Museum, Dublin you can see what are claimed to be the earliest Irish musical instruments found – twenty-six trumpets made of bronze. These date back to at least 500 BC.

According to the writings of the Irish monks of St Gall's between AD 650 and 900, there were several types of ancient instruments:

cruit and cláirseach (harp)
psalterium, nabla, timpan, kinnor, trigonon and ocht-tedach (stringed instruments)
buinne (oboe or flute)
bennbuabhal and corn (horns)
cuislenna (bagpipes)
feadán (flute or fife)
guthbuinne (horn)
stoc and sturgan (trumpets)
pípai (pipes)
craebh ciúil and crann ciúil (musical branch of cymbalum)
cnámha (castanets)
fidil (fiddle)

The professional names of the various performers were:

cruitire (harper)
timpanach (timpanist)
buinnire (flute player)
cornaire (horn player)
cuisleannach (bagpipe player)
feadánaigh (fife player)
graice (horn player)
stocaire and sturganaidhe (trumpeter)
pípaire (piper)

The Irish Harp

The earliest musical instrument described in ancient legends was the harp – every chieftain had his harper who sang and composed in his praise. The oldest wooden harp in the world, the O'Neill harp (formerly called Brian Boru's harp) is preserved in Trinity College, Dublin and can be seen by visitors to the University. It is said to be about 600 years old.

The cruit was originally a small harp plucked with the fingers. It was subsequently played with a bow and is mentioned by an Irish poet about 400 BC. The cruit was generally played resting on the knee, or sometimes placed on a table before the performer. The cláirseach, the modern form for the instrument, is found in fourteenth-century verse. It was a large harp which had 29 to 58 strings but as a rule 30; it was considered the festive harp of the chiefs, ladies and bards. The words cruit and cláirseach were seemingly interchangeable in Ireland.

In Gaelic Ireland, harpers were professional performers granted a high status in society as the musicians of the aristocracy. From at least the eleventh century they were excellently trained court musicians attached to the retinues of kings and chiefs, writing music to order. Harps were used to accompany the recitation of epic poetry, and probably performed solo pieces and songs. It was an oral tradition passed by ear from player to player and never written down. Under the Gaelic tradition, music and poetry flourished, and was protected as part of the established order.

From 1600 onwards this changed as invasions ousted the local chiefs and replaced them by Anglo-Irish aristocracy. Some harpers maintained their positions, but now with an English and European influence and bias in their music. Others became travelling musicians which led to a cross-fertilization of musical traditions and stylised music with the folk airs.

Through the seventeenth century the harp declined steadily and by the end of the eighteenth century the tradition had almost ended. The Belfast Harpers' Festival in 1792 was the last occasion in which harpers came together to play and this was the only time that their music was written down in any quantity. Only ten Irish players attended, and one Welshman.

Some of the most famous were Rory Dall O'Cahan (c. 1600), who was one of the earliest harpers of eminence, Thomas O' Connallon (c. 1650), who was said to be the greatest of harpers, and Turlough O'Carolan, who was born at Newtown, near Nobber, County Meath in 1670 and died on 25 March 1738. He was considered to be one of the best in the old Gaelic tradition and perhaps the most remembered today for more than 200 wonderful music pieces that he composed.

Today harpers are quite rare and their numbers are very low in comparison with other folk musicians. Mostly they play as solo performers and are very popular at concerts, receptions and special events.

The Pipes

Although referred to as the 'Uilleann' pipes, the correct name is 'Union'! A plausible explanation for the name 'union' derives from the act of joining the first (tenor) regulator that was added to the pipes 'in union' with the chanter.

While we know that pipes were said to be played from the earliest times, the first written mention was in the list of St Gall's in AD 650. The next mention occurs in the ninth century. It seems safe to say that the bagpipe was known in the eleventh century, as this would be in line with the history of the instrument in medieval times – by the eleventh century pipes had spread throughout western Europe. It is not until the late fifteenth or early sixteenth century that we find a crude woodcarving of a piper in Woodstock Castle, County Kilkenny.

O'Farrell provided the earliest known tutor for the instrument in his 'Collection of National Irish Music for Union Pipes' (c. 1800).

In the eighteenth and nineteenth centuries pipers travelled with the dancing masters as they toured the countryside and played the music for dance classes and also for social gatherings such as house and crossroad dances.

In recent years Leo Rowsome (1903–70) was known as king of the pipers – he was a great piper, pipe-maker and teacher. The Rowsome family has produced five generations of champion pipers, a remarkable achievement. Another piper who has parted from us in recent years is Seamus Ennis, who was a great piper, music collector, teacher and broadcaster. Paddy Moloney, also a piper, is well known to all as the leader of the Chieftains – an Irish group who are famed for their great variety of musical talents and creative compositions.

Today Liam Ó Floinn is perhaps the best known piper. While Liam has played with several groups, he has become famous purely for his solo playing. He is responsible for the high level of piping, bringing it from the small music session to the concert and state halls, where he is often accompanied by great orchestras playing extremely difficult pieces of newly composed music.

Traditional Fiddle

References to fiddles being played for dancing are not so clear. An account from the end of the seventh century tells us that the citizens of Cork in the south of Ireland, even when they could afford nothing else, brought their children up to dance, fence and play the fiddle. The fiddle is very suited to the playing of dance music and the fingering is flexible enough to permit all forms of ornamentation. By the eighteenth century its use had become universal. Today it is the one instrument which is almost always included in a band or group playing for Irish dancers. The fiddle is also the instrument most commonly used to play for Irish dance competitions.

Perhaps the greatest player of Irish dance music on the fiddle is Sean McGuire from Belfast. His music has been very popular with dancers and teachers for almost forty years.

The Flute

It is not possible to give an exact date when the flute became popular with traditional musicians in Ireland, but it is reckoned to be in the eighteenth century. You can find the instrument in many of the eighteenth-century collections of country dances, in which it was usually described as the German flute. However, it is more likely that it originated from France.

There were several different types of flutes, the older ones being single-keyed with the more modern style being a fully-keyed instrument. The older type was said to be more suitable for playing traditional music. Today the flute is one of the most important instruments in any session of Irish dance music and is a must in the line- up of any Irish traditional group.

The Whistle

There is mention of the whistle being played by Aileann, chief of the Tuatha De Danann in the period approximately 1600 BC. Feadánaigh or players of the feadán, are mentioned in ancient laws which applied to musicans who played at fairs, sports tournaments and other public meetings.

Excavations which took place in 1968 in High Street, one of the oldest parts of Dublin, unearthed several musical instruments belonging to the twelfth century. One of them was an intact whistle made of bone with two finger holes, which can be seen in the National Museum in Dublin.

Today, two types of whistles are in use by traditional musicians: one, the Clarke 'C' whistle which is made of tin and tapered with an underlip of wood set into the head; the second (and more modern) type consists of a metal column with a plastic mouthpiece.

The tin whistle is usually the first instrument to be played by newcomers to Irish music. After they get the feeling of the whistle they sometimes move on to another instrument.

My memories of great whistle players go back to Dublin in the late sixties when the traditional music and dance community was quite small and everybody knew each other. At this time I had the pleasure to know Mary Bergin, who is one of the finest whistle players a person could hope to listen to. Mary came from Blackrock, County Dublin, and today lives in the West of Ireland – as good a player today as ever she was. Another very good whistle player at that time was Helena Rowsome, daughter of Leo Rowsome, the king of the pipers, who at that time lived in Clontarf on the north side of Dublin. Today Helena lives in the North of Ireland.

Modern Instruments

Fiddle, flute and pipes were the main providers of dance music from the eighteenth century until the latter part of the nineteenth century when the melodeon was introduced to Ireland. The melodeon became very popular with dancers and the instrument was very quickly developed to the button accordion by the addition of a second row of keys. Then came the concertina from England, followed by the piano accordion.

Ceili bands came into being in the early twentieth century to cater for the big revival in Irish dancing. The instruments used in bands at this time were flute, chromatic accordion, fiddle, drums, piano, piano accordion and double bass. This is still the line-up with many bands today. Some bands in the last thirty years have introduced the banjo – this can mix very well with the other instruments and can certainly put great life into the music, which is very much appreciated by the dancers.

Today there are other stringed instruments, such as the mandolin, which have been introduced to Irish music, and also we must not forget the bodhrán. However, these are mainly used by ballad and contemporary Irish groups, and in Celtic rock.

Rhythms of Dance Music

The Jig, which is the oldest form of dance music surviving in Ireland today, can be found in three forms:

The Double Jig, which is the most commonly used for ceili dances, is played in 6/8 time The Slip Jig, which is sometimes referred to as the hop jig and is usually only danced by females, is played in 9/8 time

The Single Jig is played in 6/8 time and occasionally in 12/8 time

The Reel is played in 2/4 time

The Hornpipe is played in 4/4 time

The Polka is played in 2/4 time

The Slide is played in 12/8 time

The Fling is played in 4/4 time

Irish Dance Bands

Some of the best known and most popular Irish dance bands which I have had the pleasure to dance to are The Tulla Ceili Band and The Kilfenora Ceili Band from Clare, The Bunclody from Wexford, The Liverpool Ceili Band and the Dublin-based Eamon Ceannt and The Castle Ceili Band, who had lots of famous characters. The Simasa from Dundalk, who had many great personalities and were always a joy to listen and dance to, have been amongst the top ceili bands for the last thirty years. Sadly, their founder and leader, Rory Kennedy, has recently passed on, but members of his family are carrying on the tradition at a very high level. These bands have been playing pure Irish music between them for over fifty years and most of them are still going strong.

Other great dance bands in the last forty years were The Ardellis Ceili Band and The Donal Ring Ceili Band from Cork, The Richard Fitzgerald Ceili Band from Donegal and The Gallowglass from Naas. These last four did not only play Irish dance music, but also a variety of music for Gay Gordons, waltzes and barn dances.

Perhaps one of the greatest nights I can remember was when Jimmy Shand and his dance band from Scotland came to Dublin in the late sixties. It was without question the greatest evening of dance anyone could wish to spend – we danced for more than four hours non-stop and felt as fresh as daisies at the end because the music was so good.

Today we have some very good dance bands which are keeping up the high standards. These include The Fodhla, who have been playing all types of Irish dances in perfect rhythm for over twenty-five years. Their stage presentation is also first class – something which is lacking in so many other Irish bands. Shaskeen are a band who have made quite a few excellent recordings and their rhythm is disciplined and good to dance to. There are many other Irish music groups who often play at sessions in pubs and their music is very good.

With Irish dance music you are talking about a very specialised area – strict rhythms must be kept throughout the dance and this demands discipline on behalf of the musicians. Too often we have the experience of musicians starting at the correct tempo, but before long playing like mad at about three times the tempo they started. If you mention it to them they will tell you that is the way they play at pub sessions. So we can see that there are at least two types of music groups: ones that specialise in playing for dancing and are capable of keeping to the correct tempo (perhaps for a ceili which might last more than three hours), and ones who play at sessions in pubs and halls and may start with a jig which can drift into a reel and back to a slip jig and God knows where after that. At no time would I wish to deny Irish musicians the freedom of expression, but I feel it is important to point out the different types of music (and musicians) for the information for dancers.

Dance Competition Musicians

When it comes to playing for solo and figure dancing at exhibitions and competitions, you move into a very specialised area of music. It takes a very good musician who must have a great knowledge of Irish dance and be blessed with good patience. Not only must you play reels, jigs, hornpipes and slip jigs a hundred times over at the tempo requested by the dancers, but you must also know how to play over thirty set dances each with their own strict rhythm. For example, The Lodge Road and The Blackbird (both in 2/4 time), have fifteen bars in each step and thirty bars in the set. You must also know how to play for all the special ceili dances like The Three Tunes, Trip To The Cottage, Humours of Bandon, Lannigen's Ball and many more.

Without this dance musician you could not have a feis; neither could you perform special dance arrangements. Of all the Irish musicians, the one who plays for dance competitions and exhibitions has, in my opinion, contributed more to the development of Irish dance than any other. It would be only proper and right that we pay tribute to May Keogh from Dublin who has played at Irish dance competitions for more than fifty years. Today there are many fine musicians who play for competitions and they have produced a great variety of audio tapes and CDs which are a great assistance to teachers and students.

The Great Irish Music Collectors

The Neale Family

It was not until 1726 that a collection appeared consisting wholly of Irish music. Containing forty-nine airs, 'A Collection of The Most Celebrated Irish Tunes' was published by John and William Neale, father and son, who owned a music business at Christ Church yard, Dublin. The only surviving copy is now preserved in the collections of Edward Bunting's manuscripts at Queens University, Belfast. The Neales also published, with their proper tunes, 'A Choice Collection of Country Dances'.

The Neale family built the Crow Street Music Hall in 1731; John Neale was chairman of The Charitable Music Society, which built the new music hall in Fishamble Street where the first public performance of Handel's Messiah was given in 1742.

Edward Bunting

Edward Bunting was the first of the great collectors. He was born in the city of Armagh in 1773, the son of an Irish mother and an English father who had come to Ireland as a mining engineer. When Edward was only 11 years old, he was appointed substitute organist in a Belfast parish church. When he was 19, he had his first contact with traditional Irish music when he was appointed musical scribe for the Belfast Harpers' Festival, which was held in

1792 in the Assembly Room of the Belfast Exchange. Bunting was engaged to take down the various airs played by the different harpers and this was the beginning of his first collection.

Bunting spent his life travelling the country and collecting Irish music. He published a great number of collections – amongst them was the 1796 volume 'Edward Bunting's General Collection of Ancient Irish Music', which contained 66 airs. This was the first collection of its kind taken down by hand from the performers who played traditionally.

In 1809 he published his second volume, 'A General Collection of the Ancient Music of Ireland'. His last publication, 'Ancient Music of Ireland', was published in 1840.

Edward Bunting died in 1843 in Dublin where he had lived for several years and is buried in Mount Jerome Cemetery at Harolds Cross Park, just south of the city centre.

O'Farrell

A few years after the appearance of Bunting's first volume, a collection was published in London entitled 'O'Farrell's Collection of National Irish Music for the Union Pipes'. This was the work of O'Farrell, a piper from Clonmel in Tipperary who had settled in London.

His second work was called 'A Pocket Companion for the Irish or Union Pipes' (c. 1810). This work contained hundreds of airs and dance tunes, including the earliest version of The Fox Chase.

George Petrie

George Petrie (1789–1866) was born in Dublin of Scottish ancestry and from boyhood he was interested in Irish music. He was a distinguished antiquarian and artist, and a colleague and friend of John O'Donovan and Eugeen O'Curry, two outstanding scholars of the day.

Petrie's duties as an official of the Ordinance Survey Office gave him the opportunity to take down airs from native musicians from all parts of the country. His wish was to collect and preserve the music but he had no wish to see the results of his labour in print.

His work was published by the Society for the Preservation and Publishing of the Melodies of Ireland. The first collection, 'Ancient Music of Ireland', was published in 1855 and contained 147 airs accompanied by extensive historical and descriptive notes. A second collection of 39 airs was published in 1882, sixteen years after Petrie's death. A further selection from Petrie's manuscripts, containing over 200 airs, was edited by Francis Hoffmann in 1877.

Petrie's total manuscript collection, containing a total of 2,148 pieces, was entrusted to Sir Charles Stanford by Petrie's daughter for editing and publication. Stanford's editions appeared in three parts over the years 1902 to 1905 under the title of 'The Complete Collection of Irish Music as noted by George Petrie'.

Patrick Weston Joyce

Joyce (1827–1914), a young man from Glenosheen, County Limerick, became friends with George Petrie when Petrie was engaged in preparing his 'Ancient Music of Ireland'. At Petrie's suggestion, Joyce began to note down the music of his native county and gave freely and gladly of his material to the older man. The Stanford edition included 195 airs which Petrie had received from Joyce, the greatest single contribution to this collection.

Joyce published his own first volume of airs in 1873 called 'Ancient Irish Music', which contained 100 airs with notes, sources and other interesting information. Joyce published two other smaller works, 'Irish Music and Song' in 1887 containing twenty songs, and 'Irish Peasant Songs', which contained seven songs in English. His major work, 'Old Irish Folk Music and Songs', was published in 1909 and contained 842 airs.

Dr Henry Hudson

Dr Henry Hudson was born in 1798 in the same house in Rathfarnham where Patrick Pearse was to establish St Enda's College in 1912. Today it is a museum to honour Patrick and Willy Pearse, and is also the headquarters of The Irish National Folk Company.

Hudson compiled a considerable collection of folk music containing 870 tunes. He was also musical editor of The Citzen, a Dublin monthly magazine, in which he published, with extensive notes, selections from his own collection.

William Forde

William Forde was a well-known Cork musician who lived in the first half of the nineteenth century. He was the author and editor of several music works and lectured on music as far away as Peru and China.

His collections of Irish music were made between the years 1840 and 1850. Forde worked on a collection of over 1,800 airs and had hoped to publish his work in January 1845, but unfortunately he could not get any sponsors or patrons to fund him. He died in London five years later.

John Edward Pigot

John Pigot, son of the Lord Chief Baron of the Exchequer, shared his father's interest in music, being an accomplished performer and composer, and was the author of some stirring national songs which were published in The Nation. After Pigot came into possession of

William Forde's manuscript collection, he gathered Irish music from traditional singers and players, and his collection contains over 3,000 items.

James Goodman

James Goodman was born in 1829 in Ventry, County Kerry, the son of the Reverend Thomas Chute Goodman, Rector of Dingle. He was a native Irish speaker and an excellent performer on the pipes. On graduating from Trinity College, Dublin, where he had studied for the Church, he was appointed to a curacy near Skibbereen in County Cork.

Goodman compiled his collection during the years 1860 to 1866 – the four volumes contain a wealth of dance music and slow airs noted by Goodman himself.

For twelve years prior to his death Canon Goodman, as he was then, was Professor of Irish in Trinity College, Dublin. He died in Skibbereen in 1896 at the age of sixty-seven.

Francis O'Neill

Francis O'Neill was the greatest collector as far as dance music is concerned. Born at Tralibane in West Cork in 1849, he had a very interesting and exciting life. At the age of 16 he ran away from home to Cork City where he boarded a ship heading for Sunderland in the north of England, working his passage as payment. After serving at sea for some years and surviving a shipwreck in the mid-Pacific, he landed in San Francisco. He then worked as a shepherd, school teacher and railway worker in various parts of the United States before arriving in Chicago where he entered the police force in 1873. He became Chief Superintendent of Police in Chicago in 1901.

O'Neill had become an accomplished player of the flute by 14 years of age. Although he was responsible for the publication of thousands of airs and tunes, it seems that he was never able to commit music to paper – his keen ear and excellent memory enabled him to store the melodies in his head. It was a namesake of his in the police force, Sergeant James O'Neill, who committed to paper all the music which Francis had memorised from the playing of his parents and musicians of his native district.

O'Neill's first publication, 'The Music of Ireland', appeared in 1903. This was the biggest collection ever published – it contained 1,850 pieces including 625 airs, 75 tunes attributed to Carolan, 50 marches and a total of 1,100 dance tunes. 'The Music of Ireland' was so successful that, in response to many demands, O'Neill produced his second collection in 1907 called 'The Dance Music of Ireland', which contained 1,001 dance tunes. This second volume was also very successful and became the bible of traditional musicians.

He produced two other music collections – 'Irish Music', which contained 400 pieces, and 'Waifs and Strays of Gaelic Melody'. In Irish Folk Music, A Fascinating Hobby, published in 1910, O'Neill shares his knowledge of Irish music and musicians based on his experience while compiling his great collections.

Francis O'Neill's books on Irish dance music have never been equalled to this day and all lovers of music and dance owe so much to this man. From humble beginnings became one of the best-known personalities in the world of Irish music because of his great determination and enthusiasm for life, and his love for Ireland and its music.

Breandán Breathnach

We could not end our chapter on Irish music collectors and writers without mention of Breandán Breathnach. In his lifetime of research, writing and publishing, he has kept us all up to date on the folk music and dances of Ireland and, in so doing, bridged a gap of almost sixty years.

Breathnach was born in the Liberties of Dublin on 1 April 1912. An expert piper and chairman and founder-member of Na Piobairí Uilleann (The Association of Uilleann Pipers), he was acknowledged as one of the foremost authorities on the traditional music of Ireland.

Among his many writings and collections were Ceol Rince na hÉireann ('Folk Music and Dances of Ireland'), which was published in 1971, and also Dancing in Ireland, published in 1983. Both of these were excellent studies of the history and development of Irish traditional music, song and dance, and are the main reference materials on this subject today. Breandán was also editor and publisher of Ceol, a highly regarded magazine on Irish traditional music.

Breandán worked with the Arts Council as the Irish Traditional Music Officer for many years. Sadly it was while walking to his retirement party in the Arts Council Offices that he suffered a heart attack and died on 6 November 1985.

On his death, he left vast archives of traditional music, song and dance material. These prompted the Irish Government to set up The Irish Traditional Music Archives which makes the material available to researchers and members of the public with an interest in the subject. It is well worth a visit at 63 Merrion Square, Dublin 2 (tel: 01-6619699).

A Tribute to Teachers

Congratulations must go to teacher and adjudicator Olive Hurley from Dublin who took on the very difficult task of producing the first professional video recording of all thirty ceili dances in the Irish Dance Commission's books 1, 2 and 3. This was a personal venture and great credit is due to Olive for getting on with the task while others sat around talking about it. This work is of excellent quality and without doubt one of the most important contributions to the teaching and development of Irish dancing in the twentieth century.

The first World Ceili and Figure Dance Championship was won by the famous Cork dancing school Cullinanes in 1970 (teacher, Dr John Cullinane, Irish dance historian), and The Inis Ealga School, Dublin (teacher, Maitiu Ó Maoiléidigh) was one of the most famous Irish dancing schools in the twentieth century. The great Irish dance representatives from London – the Kavanagh Academy (teacher, Ted Kavanagh), and the Bowler Academy (teachers, Terry Bowler and his wife Nancy Brown) – would be rated amongst the top teams in the world in the twentieth century.

It is fitting that we make a special tribute to the late Mrs Matthews (Mrs M.) from Dundalk who was the most successful teacher of Irish dance champions in the twentieth century. Mrs M. trained winners at all levels and had great success in the Ulster, All Ireland and World Championships. Perhaps it is for her special talent in training so many male All Ireland and World Championship winners that she will be best remembered. She has left behind a great legacy to Irish dance and her fine teaching qualities are carried on by her many pupils who are Irish dance teachers and adjudicators today. I had the pleasure to know Mrs M. who was a kind and unassuming lady with a very good sense of humour.

The following is a roll of honour of some of the teachers/dancers who made a great contribution to Irish dancing in the twentieth century:

Essie Connolly, Lily Comerford, Maggie Kane, Cora Cadwell, Ita Cadwell, Kitty Murtagh, Evelyn O'Connor, Brenda Bastable, Eily McGann, Ma Butler, Rory O'Connor, Peter Bolton, Harry McCaffrey, Maitiu Ó Maoiléidigh, Kathleen Le Gear, Joseph and Treasa Halpin, Áine ní Thuathaigh, Tony Nolan, Thomas Cullen, Una O'Rourke, Pat Matthews, Tomás Ó Faircheallaigh, Cormac Mac Fhionnlaoich, Tom Lawlor, Bridie Clements, Monica Clerkin, Irene Lennon, Cormac O'Keeffe, George Leonard, Peggy McTeggart, Peggy Carthy, Brendan de Glin, Lillian O'More, Nan Quinn, Anna McCoy, Jerry Molyneaux, Freddie and Willie Murray, Professor Reidy, Jack O'Brien, Charlie Smythe, Betty Kelly, Ted Kavanagh, Terry Bowler, Cyril McNiff, Anna O'Sullivan, Fedelmia Davis, Peter Smith, Kevin McKenna, Jimmy Erwin, Mike Bergin, Una Ellis, Maura O'Reilly, Tessie Burke, Dennis and Margie Dennehy, Maureen McErlean, Tom Hill, Patrick Long, Professor McKenna, Professor John McNamara, Kathleen Mulkerin, Bridie McCarthy, William Healy, Ann Healy, Bill Healy, Irene Bachmann, Desmond Penrose, Maureen McTeggart, Susan Castro, Stephen Comerford, Jack Murphy, Jack Barron, Dick Sisk, Peggy Smith, Kathleen Rhondeau, Violet Moore, Mary Bastis, Paul Philip Tynan, Yvonne O'Brien, Erin O'Daly, Thelma Harris.

PART 2

A SELECTION OF THIRTY POPULAR IRISH
COMPETITION AND SOCIAL DANCES

List of Dances   # Gaelic Name

Round Dances
(1)   Two-Hand Jig   Port na Siamseí
(2)   Two-Hand Reel   Cor Beirte
(3)   The Stack of Barley   Staicín Eorna
(4)   The Big Dance   An Rince Mór
(5)   The Bonfire Dance   Rince Mór na Tiné

Long Dances/Progressive Dances
(6)   The Long Dance   Rince Fada
(7)   The Bridge of Athlone   Droichead Atha Luain
(8)   Haste to the Wedding   Deifir na Bainise
(9)   The Siege of Carrick   Briseadh na Carraige
(10)   The Antrim Reel   Cor Aontroma
(11)   The Waves of Tory   Tonnaí Thoraige
(12)   The Rakes of Mallow   Réicí Mhala
(13)   The Walls of Limerick   Ballaí Luimní
(14)   The Siege of Ennis   Ionsaí na hInse

Four-Hand Dances
(15)   The Four-Hand Reel   Cor Ceathrair
(16)   The Humours of Bandon   Pléaráca na Banndan

Six-Hand Dances
(17)   The Harvest-Time Jig   Port an Fhómhair
(18)   The Fairy Reel   Cor na Sióg
(19)   The Glencar Reel   Cor Gleann Cearr
(20)   The Duke Reel   Cor an Diúic

Eight-Hand Dances
(21)   The Cross Reel   An Cor Casta
(22)   The Sweets of May   Aoibhneas na Bealtaine
(23)   The Eight-Hand Reel   Cor Ochtair
(24)   The High Caul Cap   Cadhp an Chúil Aird
(25)   The Eight-Hand Jig   Port Ochtair
(26)   The Three Tunes   Na Tri Foinn
(27)   The Morris Reel   Cor Muirgheis

Ten-Hand Dance
(28)   The Haymakers Jig   Baint an Fhéir

Twelve-Hand Dance
(29)   Lannigan's Ball   Bainéis Uí Lonagáin

Sixteen-Hand Dance
(30)   The Sixteen-Hand Reel   Cor Sé Dhuiné Dhé

Guide To Dance Formations

KEY -

= Woman

= Man

This is the line-up formation of most dances

Round Dances

Two-Hand Dances

Four-Hand Dances

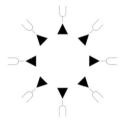

Eight-Hand Dances

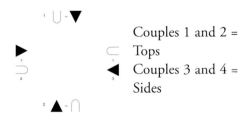

Couples 1 and 2 = Tops
Couples 3 and 4 = Sides

Long and Progressive Dances

Four-Hand Dances

1 + 3 = Leading Couple
2 + 4 = Opposite Couple

Six-Hand Dances

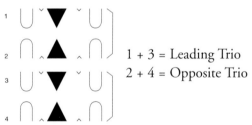

1 + 3 = Leading Trio
2 + 4 = Opposite Trio

Eight-Hand Dances

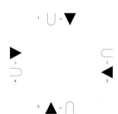

1, 2, 5, 6 = Leading Four
3, 4, 7, 8 = Opposite Four

Sixteen-Hand Dances

1 = Leading Couple

Ten-Hand Dances

Couple 1 + 2 = First To[p]
Couple 3 + 4 = First Si[de]
Couple 5 + 6 = Second [Top]
Couple 7 + 8 = Second [Side]

Explanations of common terminology and often used movements

The Body

The Body is the main part of most Four-, Six-, Eight-, and Sixteen-Hand Dances comprising of several movements which are usually repeated several times. The main difference between dances is the Body, as often Figures are repeated in several dances but the Body of each dance has its own distinct movements which are always different to those of other dances.

The Figures

Figures are parts of the dance which are danced in between the Body in Four-, Six-, Eight- and Sixteen-Hand Dances. The normal pattern is Body, Figure, Body, Figure, Body, Figure and Body. There are normally three Figures in each dance. Each Figure in a dance has different patterns.

Round Dances – Long Dances – Progressive Dances

These dances are the least difficult of all the dances. They are made up of a pattern of between four and six movements for each dance which are repeated many times with the same partner in Two-Hand Dances and are repeated with new couples as dancers progress in Progressive Long Dances.

Tops and Sides

Tops and Sides are the terms used to make the dance formation and the order in which movements should be danced.

Leading Tops

The couple with their backs to the music or top of the hall. Leading Tops are always the couple to perform the Figure of the dance first and are called couple number 1.

Opposite Tops

The couple facing Leading Tops, the music and the top of the hall. They usually perform the Figures second and are called couple number 2.

Leading Sides

The couple which are positioned on the left side of the set to Leading Tops. They are called couple number 3 and dance the Figures third in the set.

Opposite Sides

The couple which are positioned on the right side of Leading Tops. They are called couple number 4 and are the last couple to dance the Figures in an Eight-Hand Dance.

Lead Around

Lead Around is danced at the beginning and end of many dances. In an Eight-Hand Dance it consists of eight Promenade Steps in a circle to the right (anti-clockwise) and eight Promenade Steps in a circle to the left (clockwise) danced by all the couples in the set.

Advance and Retire

The term used when the dance movement requires couples to move forward and back.

Dance Around

The term Dance Around means dancers should take partners' both hands and dance around in an anti-clockwise direction – in most figures you dance eight steps in a complete circle around the opposite couple. When Dance Around comes at the end of a dance all dance anti-clockwise around the outside of the complete set and repeat this movement back clockwise to starting position.

Today the movement Dance Around, when it applies to the end of a dance – for example in The Walls of Limerick or during The Haymakers Jig – is more commonly danced at ceilis as a swing.

Side Step (often referred to as Sides)

The Side Step is the most important movement in ceili figure dances and must be mastered before the dancer can perform any of the dances with any degree of grace or satisfaction. Dancers should practise the Side Step in several directions until they feel comfortable and confident when dancing with others.

Two Short Threes

Two Short Threes are danced at the end of a reel Side Step and often throughout many dances.

The Rising Step (also referred to as Rise and Grind)

The Rising Step is danced in jigs at the end of a Side Step and on other occasions in dances danced in jig time.

The Sink and Grind

The Sink and Grind is performed in dances in jig time – it differs from the Rise and Grind in that you do not rise your foot but sink your foot or keep the movement low. Usually the Sink and Grind is repeated twice on the same foot.

Hands Across

This is an often used movement where dancers put their right hand into the centre and dance four Promenade Steps clockwise and then turn and place their left hand into the centre and dance four Promenade Steps anti-clockwise back to their own place. This movement can also be referred to as The Wheel or The Mill.

Full Chain

The Full Chain is danced by facing partners. Gents turn to the right and ladies turn to the left – they give each other right hands and start to chain on to the next lady and gent giving them left hands. Gent anti-clockwise and lady clockwise, they continue the chain giving right and left hands alternately until they meet up with each other again in starting positions.

Half Chain

The Half Chain is danced by facing partners. Gents turn to the right and ladies turn to the left, they give each other right hands and start to chain on to the next lady and gent giving them left hands. Gent anti-clockwise and lady clockwise, they continue the chain giving right and left hands alternately until they meet up with each other again half-way around the set. They then take partners' two hands in crossed hand position, right hand in right hand and left hand in left hand, and Lead Around to place in the direction the man was dancing anti-clockwise.

Double Quarter Chain

Gent takes partner's right hand in his right and both turn once in place, gent chains with left hand to lady on his left, both turn in place, he then chains back to his partner with his right hand turning her in place. He then continues on to the lady on his right – giving her his left hand they both turn in place. He then chains back to his own partner with his right hand and both turn once into place.

Ladies Chain

This is a Figure used in several dances. Ladies advance, giving right hand to each other in the centre and continue on to the opposite gent giving them their left hand while both turn anti-clockwise in place. Ladies return to their own partner giving them their right hand and they make a full turn in place. Both couples now dance a complete circle around each other (Dance Around).

Return Chain

The Return Chain is danced by facing partners. Gents turn to the right and ladies turn to the left – they give each other right hands and start to chain on to the next lady and gent giving them left hands. Gent anti-clockwise and lady clockwise, they continue the chain giving right and left hands alternately until they meet up with each other again with right hands halfway around the set. They make a full turn around and chain back to their original position meeting each other with right hands and turning into place.

Instructions For Hand And Arm Positions

Standard Dancing Position

Gent takes lady's left hand in his right.
Hold hands at shoulder height.
Keep elbows and arms close together.
Keep outside hands straight and relaxed by the side.

Crossed Hands Position for Lead Around etc.

Gent takes lady's right hand in his right hand and the lady's left hand in his left hand.
Gent's right hand should be over lady's left hand.
Both hands should be held at chest height.

Dance Around with Crossed Hands

Gent holds lady's left hand in his left hand and the lady's right hand in his right hand.
The right hands should be on top.
Hands should be held at shoulder height with the arms close to the body relaxed.

The Swing

Gent puts his right hand under the lady's left arm and places it on her waist.

Lady puts her right hand under the gent's left arm and places it on his waist.

Gent holds lady's left hand in his left under their right arms.

Right Hands Across in the Centre (also called The Wheel or The Mill)

Gents give right hand across in the centre to opposite gent.

Ladies give right hands across into the centre and place their hands on top of the gents' hands.

Hands should be held at shoulder height.

Instructions for Steps

Instructions for Steps
The Side Step
Movement – The Side Step to the right is danced as follows:

Starting Position – The dancer should stand with weight balanced on both feet and heels together.

(1) Hop lightly with the weight balanced on the ball of the left foot and the right foot slightly forward, toe pointing towards the right.

1

(2) Move the right foot towards the right at the second beat of the music, at the same time transferring the weight from the left foot to the right foot.

2

(3) Bring the toe of the left foot to the heel of the right, transferring the weight from the right foot to the left.

3

4

(4) Move the right foot towards the right at the fourth beat of the music, at the same time transferring the weight from the left foot to the right.

5

(5) Bring the toe of the left foot to the heel of the right foot, at the same time transferring the weight from the right foot to the left.

6

(6) Move the right foot towards the right at the sixth beat, at the same time transferring the weight from the left foot to the right.

7

(7) Bring the toe of the left foot to the heel of the right foot, at the same time transferring the weight from the right foot to the left.

The Side Step is followed in reel time by the Two Short Threes and in jig time usually by the Rising Step or the Sink and Grind.

The Two Short Threes

1 A

Starting Position – Place weight on left foot which is placed behind the heel of the right foot.

(1) Hop on left foot at the same time bringing the right foot behind the left foot and transferring weight to the right foot while raising the left foot off the ground.

1 B

1 C

2

(2) Transfer weight to the left foot at the same time raising the right foot behind.

3

(3) Place right foot to the ground and transfer weight to the right foot.

4 A

(4) Hop on the right foot at the same time bringing the left foot behind the right foot and transferring the weight to the left foot while raising the right foot off the ground.

4 B

4 C

5

(5) Transfer weight to the right foot at the same time raising the left foot off the ground.

6

(6) Place left foot behind to the ground and transfer weight to the left foot.

The Two Threes are danced at the end of the Side Step and throughout most dances.

Promenade Step

1

Starting Position – Stand with weight comfortably balanced on both feet. Heels together.

(1) Hop lightly on the left foot with the weight balanced on the ball of the left foot, at the same time raise your right foot bending at the knee.

2

(2) Moving forward place your right foot forward on the ground, transferring the weight from your left foot to your right foot at the same time raising your left foot slightly off the ground.

3

(3) Bring your left foot behind your right foot and transfer your weight onto your left foot.

4

(4) Moving forward transfer your weight back onto your right foot raising your left foot behind in preperation to commence step on left foot.

Next you start the step again repeating 1 to 4 above, but this time starting by hopping on your right foot.

The Rising Step (Jig)

1

(1) Hop on the left foot while raising the right foot in front with toe pointed.

2

(2) Hop again on left foot while bringing right foot to the rear.

3

(3) Place right foot behind left, transferring weight from left foot to right foot.

4

(4) Hop on right foot while bringing left foot behind.

5

(5) Place left foot behind right foot at the same time raising right foot.

6

(6) Place right foot down again.

7

(7) Place left foot behind right foot while raising right foot.

(8) Place right foot down again.

8

Sink and Grind (Jig)

1

(1) Jump on both feet together, the right foot in front of the left.

2

(2) Hop on left foot, raising right foot in front.

3

(3) Hop on left foot, bringing right foot behind.

4

(4) Place right foot behind left while lifting left a little off the ground.

5

(5) Transfer weight to left foot.

6

(6) Place right foot behind left while lifting left a little off the ground.

(7) Transfer weight to the left foot.

7

Two-Hand Jig – Round Dance
A very popular couple dance.

Music – Double jig.

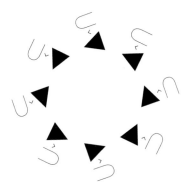

Formation – Any number of couples in a circle. Gents on the inside. Gents' right side to ladies left. Face in anti-clockwise direction.

Steps –Walking Step, Promenade Step, Side Step, Rise and Grind, Threes.

Dance Movements		
	A. Walking Steps	= 4 Bars
	B. Advance and Retire	= 4 Bars
	C. Side Step	= 8 Bars
	D. Walking Steps	= 4 Bars
	E. Advance and Retire	= 4 Bars
	F. Side Step	= 8 Bars
	G. Lead Round	= 8 Bars

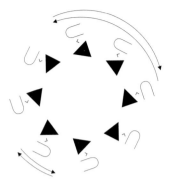

(A) Walking Step

Couple line up, gent on the inside, lady on the outside.
Gent takes partner's left hand in his right.
All couples face in the anti-clockwise direction.
Starting on the right foot both dancers take two Walking Steps forward and end with one Short Three.
Leading with their left foot they take two Walking Steps backwards and end with one Short Three (1-2-3).

(B) Advance and Retire

The dancers starting with their right foot now dance forward with two Promenade Steps, and retire back to position with two Promenade Steps.

(C) Side Step

Couples now side step to their left into the centre.
Couples now dance the Rise and Grind with their left foot.
They now side step to the right back to place and dance the Rise and Grind.
While dancing the Grind the couple about turning inwards, gent clockwise, lady anti-clockwise, and face the opposite direction (clockwise) to their starting position.

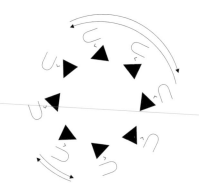

The dance is now repeated in the opposite direction.

(D) Walking Steps
Couples line up, gent on the inside, lady on the outside.
Gent takes partner's left hand in his right.
All couples face in the anti-clockwise direction.
Starting on the right foot both dancers take two Walking Steps forward and end with one Short Three.
Leading with their left foot they take two Walking Steps backwards and end with one Short Three (1-2-3).

(E) Advance and Retire
The dancers starting with their right foot now dance forward with two Promenade Steps and retire back to position with two Promenade Steps.

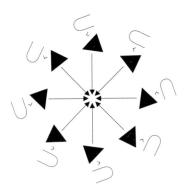

(F) Side Step
Couples now side step to their right into the centre.
Couples now dance the Rise and Grind with their right foot.
They now side step to the left back to place and dance the Rise and Grind, about turning on the Grind to leave them in their original starting position.

(G) Lead Round

All couples now take crossed hands in front, right hand in right and left in left.

The dancers dance eight Promenade Steps around the floor in an anti-clockwise direction.

Two-Hand Reel – Round Dance

One of the most popular ceili dances to dance with a good partner and plenty of floor space.

Music – Reels

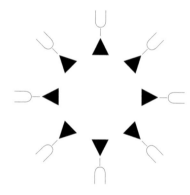

Formation – Any number of couples in a circle, gents on the inside facing partners.

Steps – Side Step, Promenade Step, Sink and Grind (Reel Time)

Dance Movements

A. Side Step   = 8 Bars
B. Change Places   = 8 Bars
C. Lead Round   = 8 Bars

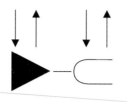

(A) Side Step

Gent faces partner.

Gent on the inside, lady on the outside.

Both take right hands and side step to the gent's left, ending with two Short Threes.

They now side step to the gent's right, ending in place with two Short Threes.

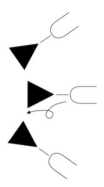

(B) Change Places

Still holding right hands the couple dance the Sink and Grind on their right foot.

The gent then makes an arch by raising his right hand and the lady dances under turning anti-clockwise with two Promenade Steps.

At the same time the gent dances into his partner's position dancing two Promenade Steps.

The gents are now on the outside and the ladies are on the inside.

They again dance the Sink and Grind but this time with the left foot.

The gent again raises his right hand to make an arch with his partner, the lady turns under the gent's arm and the gent dances back to his original position, both dancing two Promenade Steps.

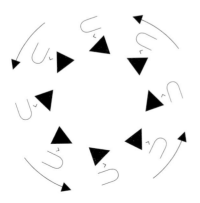

(C) Lead Round

Both dancers turn, gent to left and lady to right of starting position, to face in the same direction.

The couple now take crossed hands, right hand in right, left hand in left.

They now dance eight Promenade Steps around the hall in an anti-clockwise direction.

The dance is now repeated from the beginning and can be danced as often as desired.

The Stack of Barley – Round Dance

This is a wonderful Two-Hand Hornpipe which is a very popular dance and gives the dancers the opportunity to use all the floor space and stretch the legs.

Music – Hornpipes.

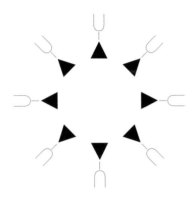

Formation – Any number of couples in a circle. Gents on the inside, ladies on the outside.

Couples face each other and hold right hand in right.

Steps – Sevens, Hornpipe Step.

Dance Movements

A. Rings = 8 Bars
B. Dance into Centre = 4 Bars
C. Dance Around = 4 Bars

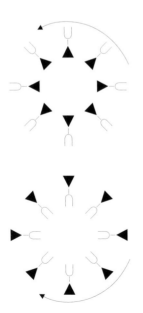

(A) Rings

This movement is made up of four Sevens, and is danced in a circle on the outside of the floor.

Couples change place at the end of each Seven.

Couples holding right hand in right hand (1st Seven), gent on the inside, side step to the gent's left.

At the end of the Side Step as they hop to start another seven (2nd seven), the gent turns to the outside and the lady to the inside.

At the start of the 3rd seven the gent turns to the inside and the lady to the outside.

As the couple start the 4th seven the gent turns to the outside and the lady turns to the inside.

At the completion of the four Sevens, the gent is on the outside and the lady on the inside.

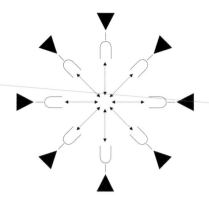

(B) Dance into Centre

All couples take crossed hands and hold them shoulder high.

The ladies have their back to the centre and the gents are facing the centre.

The gents dance two Promenade Steps forward and the ladies dance two Promenade Steps back towards the centre of the group.

The gents now dance two steps back while the ladies now dance two steps forward.

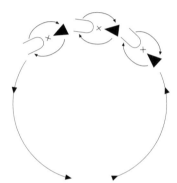

(C) Dance Around

All couples now dance around clockwise in an anti-clockwise direction moving around the hall with four Promenade Steps.

Dancers now line up in starting position to recommence dance.

An Rince Mór – Round Dance

A Round Dance for any number of couples.

Music – Reels.

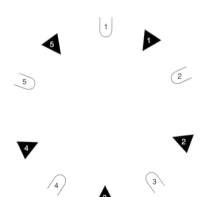

Formation – The dancers form a large ring round the room, each gent having his partner at his right hand.

Steps – Promenade Step, Side Step, Threes.

Dance Movements

A. Ring to Left and Right	= 8 Bars
B. Swing with Ladies on Left	= 8 Bars
C. Swing with Partners	= 8 Bars
D. Link Arms	= 8 Bars
E. Lead Around	= 8 Bars

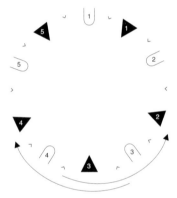

(A) Ring to Left and Right

All the dancers in ring hold hands, and side step to left, finishing with two Short Threes, and side step to the right finishing with two Short Threes.

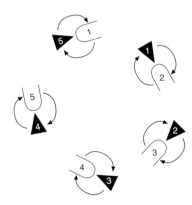

(B) Swing with Ladies on Left

Gents take crossed hands of ladies on their left, and couples swing in place clockwise.

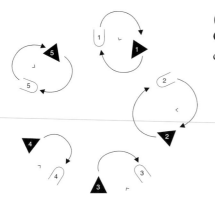

(C) Swing with Partners

Gent takes own partner's hands and swings in place clockwise.

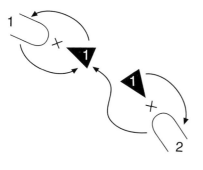

(D) Link Arms

Gents link right arms in right arms of ladies on their left and turn clockwise.

They then link left arm in left arm of partner and turn anti-clockwise.

They repeat the right arm link and turn with ladies on left.

Chain back to their partner and take both hands.

Turn her so that gent is on inside of ring and the lady is on the outside in preparation for next movement.

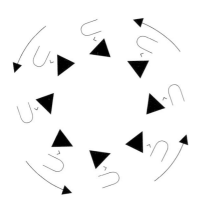

E) Lead Around

Couples lead around anti-clockwise, with Promenade Step for six bars of music, and during the last two bars form a large ring to recommence dance.

The Bonfire Dance – Round Dance

This is a dance for any number of couples, but preferably for not fewer than six. It was said to have been danced around the bonfire on St John's Eve.

Music – Reels.

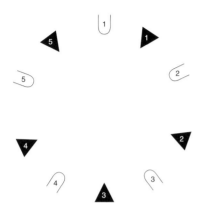

Formation – All stand in a ring facing centre, gents on the left of ladies.

Steps – Promenade Step, Side Step, Threes.

Dance Movements

A. Advance and Retire	= 8 Bars
B. Rings	= 8 Bar
C. Advance and Retire	= 8 Bars
D. Rings	= 8 Bars
E. Side Step In and Out	= 4 Bars
F. Link Arms	= 4 Bars
G. Side Step In and Out	= 4 Bars
H. Link Arms	= 4 Bars
I. The Rose	= 32 Bars
J. Swing and Exchange	= 8 Bars

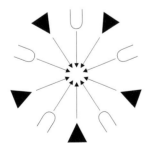

(A) Advance and Retire
All join hands and advance towards the centre with four Promenade Steps.
All retire to place with four Promenade Steps.

(B) Rings

Still holding hands all side step to the right (anti-clockwise) ending with two Short Threes.

All now side step back to the left (clockwise) back to places ending with two Short Threes.

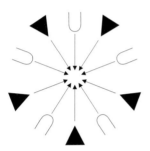

(C) Advance and Retire

All advance towards the centre with four Promenade Steps.

All retire to place with four Promenade Steps.

(D) Rings

Still holding hands all side step to the left (clockwise) ending with two Short Threes.

All now side step back to the right (anti-clockwise) back to places ending with two Short Threes.

On the last Three, partners turn to face each other.

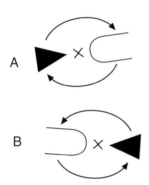

(E) Side Step In and Out
From this new position, all side step to their right, the ladies towards the centre and the gents outwards. Without doing Threes, all side step back to places.

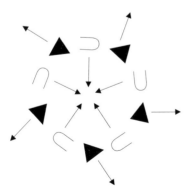

(F) Link Arms
Linking right arms partners dance two Promenade Steps clockwise, to partner's place.
Release arms.
Link left arms and return anti-clockwise with two Promenade Steps to face each other as before.

(G) Side Step In and Out
From this new position, all side step to their left, the gents towards the centre and the ladies outwards. Without doing Threes, all side step back to places.

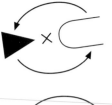

(H) Link Arms

Linking left arms partners dance two promenade steps anti-clockwise to partner's place.

Release arms.

Link right arms and return with two Promenade Steps clockwise.

All finish facing the centre of the ring.

(I) The Rose

The ladies advance slowly towards the centre with four Promenade Steps.

The ladies take hands in a ring on the fourth Three.

They now side step to the right (anti-clockwise) ending with two Threes.

On the last two Threes they turn right to face outwards, rejoining hands in a 'back to back' circle.

They side step to the left (clockwise) ending with two Short Threes.

During this twelve bars the gents have remained stationary with left hand on hip and right toe pointed slightly forward.

Ladies now advance towards partners both taking right hand and turn clockwise into position.

While ladies remain stationary, with left hand on hip and right toe forwards, the gents perform the Rose.

The gents advance slowly towards the centre with four Promenade Steps.

The gents take hands in a ring on the fourth Three.

They now side step to the left (clockwise) ending with two Threes.

On the last two Threes they turn right to face outwards, rejoining hands in 'back to back' circle.

They side step to the right (anti-clockwise) ending with two Short Threes.

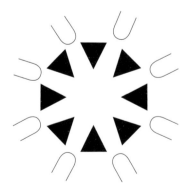

Gents now advance towards partners both taking right hand and turn clockwise into position.

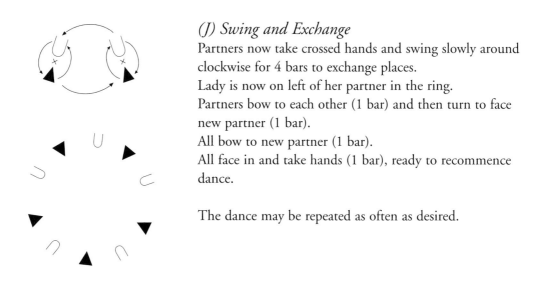

(J) Swing and Exchange

Partners now take crossed hands and swing slowly around clockwise for 4 bars to exchange places.

Lady is now on left of her partner in the ring.

Partners bow to each other (1 bar) and then turn to face new partner (1 bar).

All bow to new partner (1 bar).

All face in and take hands (1 bar), ready to recommence dance.

The dance may be repeated as often as desired.

The Rince Fada – Progressive Long Dance

Music – Double jig.

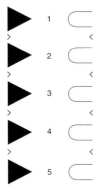

Formation – Any number of couples form up in two lines, the gents in one line, the ladies in the other, partners facing each other, gents' left side to the top of the room. Couples are numbered off from the top.

Each odd couple and the even couple immediately below them form a set.

Steps – Rising Step, Promenade Step, Side Step.

Dance Movements		
	A. Rising Step	= 4 Bars
	B. Right Wheel	= 4 Bars
	C. Rising Step	= 4 Bars
	D. Left Wheel	= 4 Bars
	E. Advance down Centre	= 8 Bars
	F. Dance Around	= 8 Bars

The Complete Guide to Irish Dance | *Frank Whelan*

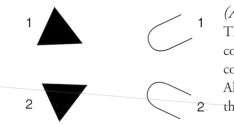

(A) Rising Step

The lady of each odd couple and the gent of the next couple below face each other, as do the gent of the odd couple and the lady of the next couple below.

All dance Rise and Grind, first on the right foot then on the left.

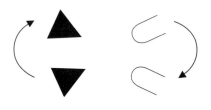

(B) Right Wheel

Each set of four join their right hands in centre, the ladies' hands above the gents', and dance clockwise with Promenade Step to places.

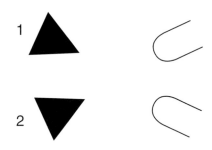

(C) Rising Step

The lady of each odd couple and the gent of the next couple below face each other, as do the gent of the odd couple and the lady of the next couple below.

All dance Rise and Grind, first on the left foot then on the right.

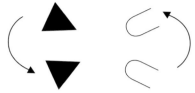

(D) Left Wheel

Each set of four join their left hands in centre, the ladies' hands above the gents', and dance anti-clockwise with Promenade Step to places.

(E) Advance Down Centre

The gents of odd couples take partners' right hands in their left while even couples stand in places.

Odd couples then advance down the centre between the even couples, with Promenade Step.

Release hands and reverse.

Take inside hands and advance back to places.

Odd couples now 'cast off'. For example, the gent passes round, and takes place below the even gent of his set, while lady passes out and round the corresponding lady, and takes place below her.

(F) Dance Around

Odd couples are now below the even couples with whom they are dancing, and from here partners take crossed hands and couples swing around each other anti-clockwise and back to these new positions.

The dance is now repeated, couple 1 dancing with couple 4, couple 3 with couple 6, and so on.

Each even couple who reaches the top and each odd couple who reaches the bottom of the line, stand idle during one complete movement of the dance.

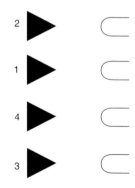

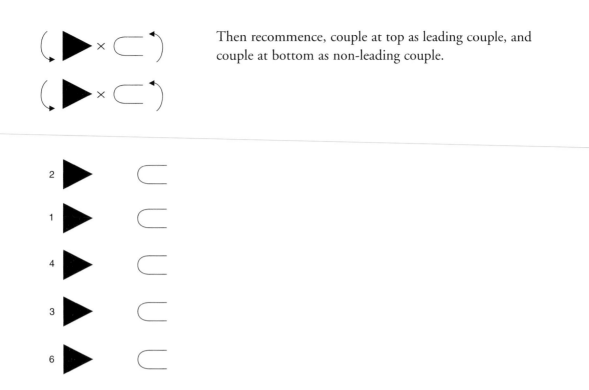

Then recommence, couple at top as leading couple, and couple at bottom as non-leading couple.

The Bridge of Athlone – A Long Dance

This is a dance from Athlone which is a town in the centre of Ireland on the road to the west from Dublin to Galway.

Music – Double jig.

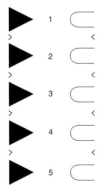

Formation – Any number of couples form up in two lines. Gents in one line, the ladies in the other. Partners facing each other. Gents' left side to the top of the room. Couples are numbered off from the top, each odd couple and the even couple immediately below them form a set.

Steps – Promenade Step, Side Step, Rising Step, Threes.

Dance Movements	A. Rising Step, Advance and Retire	= 32 Bars
	B. Down the Centre	= 8 Bars
	C. Cast Off	Depends on how many dancers
	D. The Bridge	Depends on how many dancers

(A) Rising Step, Advance and Retire

Each line of dancers hold hands and all dance Rising Step twice, beginning on the right foot.

The lines of dancers now advance and retire once, with Promenade Step.

All again dance Rising Step twice, then release hands, advance and pass through, by partners' right, to opposite side, and turn right to face back.

Repeat all above, crossing back to places, and finishing in original positions.

(B) Down the Centre

Couple 1 (sometimes the first three or five couples if the line is a long one) take right hands and side step down the centre between the two lines, finishing with two Short Threes; side step back to places, finishing as before. While they are dancing this, all the other dancers in the line stand in places.

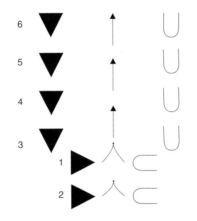

(C) Cast Off

Leading couple (or couples) now cast off, followed by all the dancers in the line, the ladies promenading outside their line and dancing down towards the opposite end of the line, the gents dancing in a similar manner on their side.

(D) The Bridge

When the couples who have done movement (B) reach the end of the line, they turn in to meet, dance a little way up, with inside hands joined, and then form an arch by joining both hands and holding them in a raised position.

The dancers following them pass underneath the arch and return to the top of the set, forming into two lines as at the beginning of the dance.

When they reach their places they form a 'bridge' by joining both hands with partner (uncrossed) and holding them in raised position.

The leading couple now release hands and dance to the top of the set, the lady passing under the 'bridge', the gent passing outside.

When they reach the top they dance back again, the gent this time passing under the 'bridge', while the lady passes outside it.

On reaching the bottom of the set they form up at the end of the lines, and the other dancers release partners' hands.

The dance is now repeated, the couple now at the top of the set leading.

Haste to the Wedding – Long Dance

This is another Long Dance for any number of couples.

Music – Double jig time, danced to the tune of the same name.

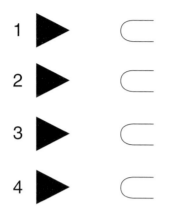

Formation – Couples are numbered off from the top. Each odd couple and the even couple immediately below them form a set. In this dance the even couples are the leading ones.

Steps – Rising Step, Side Step, Promenade Step.

Dance Movements		
	A. Rising Step	= 4 Bars
	B. Right Wheel	= 4 Bars
	C. Rising Step	= 4 Bars
	D. Left Wheel	= 4 Bars
	E. Up the Centre	= 4 Bars
	F. First Ring	= 4 Bars
	G. Second Ring	= 4 Bars
	H. Line Up	= 8 Bars

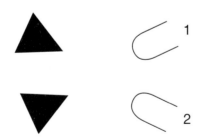

(A) Rising Step
The lady of each odd couple and the gent of the next couple below face each other, as do the gent of the odd couple and the lady of the next couple below.
All dance Rise and Grind, first on the right foot then on the left.

(B) Right Wheel

Each set of four join their right hands in centre, the ladies' hands above the gents', and dance clockwise with Promenade Step to places.

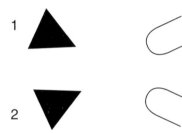

(C) Rising Step

The lady of each odd couple and the gent of the next couple below face each other, as do the gent of the odd couple and the lady of the next couple below.

All dance Rise and Grind, first on the left foot, then on the right.

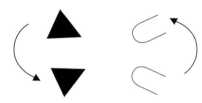

(D) Left Wheel

Each set of four join their left hands in centre, the ladies' hands above the gents', and dance anti-clockwise with Promenade Step to places.

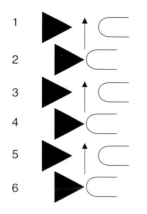

(E) Up the Centre

The even couples or leading couples take hands and side step up between the odd couples of their set, i.e. to the gents' left, finishing with two Short Threes.

Then they side step back to places, finishing as before, but on the second Three the even couple take the lady of the odd couple into a ring by joining hands (ladies of even couples being on the right of their partners ring).

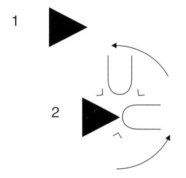

(F) First Ring

The rings of three now dance a Side Step to their right. While the even couples dance two Threes they raise their joined hands to form an arch and allow the lady of the odd couple to pass under the arch to her original position, and prepare to take her partner into the ring.

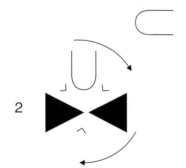

(G) Second Ring

The couple now take in the gent who has been standing idle and, joining hands with him, the three dance a Side Step to the left, and allow the gent to pass under the arch to his place while they dance two Threes.

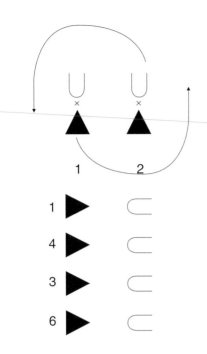

(H) Line Up

Each even couple and the odd couple next above them now swing out, and round each other, with Promenade Step, and so exchange places.

The dance is now repeated, those at either end of the line standing idle, while couple 4 dances with couple 1 and couple 6 with couple 3, and so on. On the next repetition of the dance all couples will be dancing again.

The Siege of Carrick – Progressive Long Dance

This dance was originally a Four-Hand Dance, its four movements being repeated as often as desired. It is now usually done as a Progressive Long Dance, and is so described below.

Music – Double jig. The dance is performed to the tune 'Haste to the Wedding'. Each part of the tune must be played twice after the dance commences so that the claps in C and D will fit properly to the music.

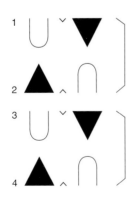

Formation – Two face two.

Steps – Promenade Step, Side Step, Dance Around.

Dance Movements		
A. Rings	= 8 Bars
B. Right and Left Wheels	= 8 Bar
C. Down Centre and Turn	= 8 Bars
D. Up Centre and Swing	= 8 Bars

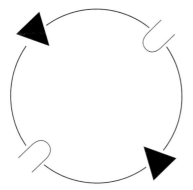

(A) Rings
Each set of four dancers hold hands to form a ring.
All dance side step to left finishing with two Short
Threes, and return to the right, finishing with two Short
Threes.

(B) Right and Left Wheels
The four now give right hands across centre, shoulder
high, with ladies' hands above gents', and dance around
clockwise, with Promenade Step.
On fourth bar all release hands and turn.
All now give left hands across and dance back to places
anti-clockwise.

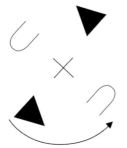

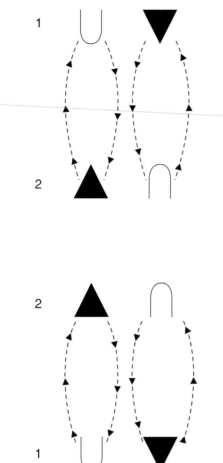

(C) Down Centre and Turn

Leading and opposite couples of each set advance to each other's places, without taking hands, leading couple passing between the opposite couple.

All retire without turning, but this time opposite couple pass between top couple.

All clap hands together twice to one bar of music, and then hook right arms and turn once in place.

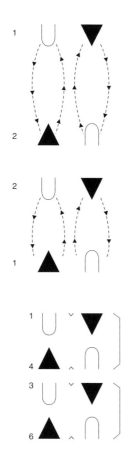

(D) Up Centre and Swing

Couples again advance, but this time opposite couple pass through.

On retiring as before, leading couple pass between the other two dancers.

All clap again twice to one bar of music, then hook right arms again, but this time they swing out, change places and progress on to the next couple.

Couple 1 now faces couple 4, and couple 3 faces couple 6, and so on, and from these new positions the dance is recommenced.

The Antrim Reel – Progressive Long Dance

Music – Reels.

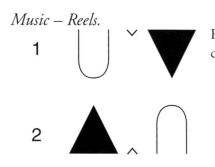

Formation – Two face two, a dance for any number of couples

Steps – Promenade Step, Side Step, two Short Threes.

Dance Movements

A. Advance and Return	= 4 Bars
B. Right and Left Half-turn	= 4 Bars

C. Side Step and Heyes	= 16 Bars
D. Dance Down Centre	= 8 Bars
E. Right and Left Wheels	= 8 Bars
F. Side Step with Opposite	= 8 Bars
G. Left and Right Wheels	= 8 Bars
H. Swing out to Next Couple	= 8 Bars

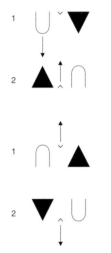

(A) Advance and Return

Couples take inside hands and advance towards each other with Promenade Step.

On second Three, release hands and reverse, turning towards each other in doing so.

Couples take inside hands and return to places, releasing hands on second Three and facing each other.

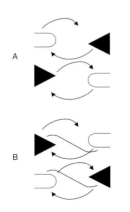

(B) Right and Left Half-turn

Partners take right hands and with Promenade Step exchange places and release hands.

Take left hands and dance back to own places.

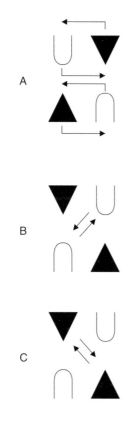

(C) Side Step and Exchange Places with Opposites (Heyes)

Partners change places with Side Step, gents passing behind ladies; all finish with two Short Threes.

The two ladies of each set change places with the Promenade Step, passing left shoulder to left shoulder, while the gents dance two Short Threes.

The ladies now dance two Short Threes while the gents change places with Promenade Step, passing right shoulder to right shoulder.

This whole movement is repeated to return to places, when crossing ladies will now cross right shoulder to right shoulder and men left shoulder to left shoulder.

(D) Dance Down Centre

All dancers face partners.

Odd couples side step to places of even couples in set, while even couples dance outside them in opposite direction. All dance two Short Threes, and on second Three odd couples release hands and fall back, while even couples advance towards partners and take hands.

From these positions all side step back to places (even couples passing between odd couples of set), and finish with two Short Threes. On second Three all fall back to original positions.

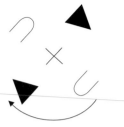

(E) Right and Left Wheels

Each set of four dancers give right hands across in centre, shoulder high, with ladies' hands above gents', and dance around clockwise.

On fourth bar all release hands and reverse.

All now give left hands across and dance back to places.

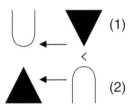

(F) Side Step with Opposite

This movement is similar to (D) above, except that gent of odd couple takes hands of lady of even couple and they dance across between the other two of set as they side step past them, this second couple taking hands to return to places with Side Step and two Threes.

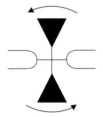

(G) Left and Right Wheels

Each set of four dancers give left hands across in centre, shoulder high, with ladies' hands above gents', and dance around anti-clockwise.

On fourth bar all release hands and turn.

All now give right hands across and dance clockwise back to places.

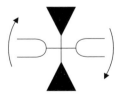

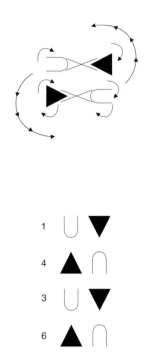

(H) Swing Out to Next Couple

Partners face each other and, taking both hands crossed, odd couples swing to right to places of even couples and vice versa. Each couple is now back-to-back with couple with whom they have been dancing, and prepare to dance with next couple.

All the above movements are now repeated, couple 1 dancing with couple 4, and couple 3 with couple 6, and so on. The dance is progressive, each odd couple moving down one position after completing all the movements, and each even couple moving up one position towards the top of the set. As each couple reaches either end of the line they stand idle during one repetition of the dance.

The Waves of Tory – Progressive Long Dance

This is a dance from Donegal, a county in the north-west of Ireland. The 'waves' in this dance are meant to represent the waves so frequently seen around the island of Tory off the north coast of Donegal.

Music – Movements A-B-C-D in reel time; E-F-G are usually done to march time.

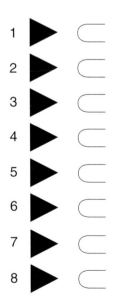

Formation – This is a dance for any number of couples in sets of four. Gents line up with their left shoulder facing the top of the hall. Ladies line up opposite their partners with their right shoulder facing the top of the hall. Top set are the first two couples at the top of the line.

Steps – Promenade Step, Marching Step.

Dance Movements	A. Advance and Retire	= 8 Bars
	B. Right and Left Hands Across	= 8 Bars
	C. Advance and Retire	= 8 Bars
	D. Left and Right Hands Across	= 8 Bars
	E. Lead off to Right and up the Centre	Depends on number of dancers
	F. The Waves	Depends on numbers of dancers
	G. Cast Off	Depends on numbers of dancers

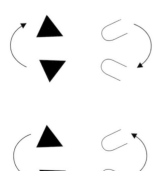

(A) Advance and Retire
The two lines advance towards each other with two Promenade Steps and retire to place with two Promenade Steps.
The two lines then advance and retire once more.

(B) Right and Left Hands Across
Each set of four dancers gives right hand across in the centre, shoulder high, and dances around clockwise with four Promenade Steps.
On the last Three they release hands and turn in.
They now give left hands across and dance around anti-clockwise, to finish in starting lines again.

(C) Advance and Retire

The two lines advance towards each other with two Promenade Steps and retire to place with two Promenade Steps.

The two lines then advance and retire once more.

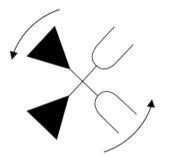

(D) Left and Right Hands Across

Each set of four dancers gives left hand across in the centre, shoulder high, and dance around anti-clockwise with four Promenade Steps.

On the last Three they release hands and turn in. They now give right hands across and dance around clockwise, to finish in starting lines again.

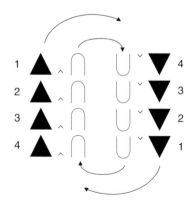

(E) Lead off to Right and up the Centre

(Note: This movement and the following movements are usually done to march time music.)

All couples turn to gents' left and take inside hands.

Couple 1 lead off to the right and down to the bottom of the set followed by the other couples.

Couple 1 turn right again and lead up the centre to place, the other couples following.

The Complete Guide to Irish Dance | *Frank Whelan*

(F) The Waves

Couple 1 release hands, turn in to each other, then face down the hall, take inside hands and raise them to form an arch and promenade towards couple 2, who pass under the arch made by couple 1.

Couple 1 now continue up the line to pass under the arch made by couple 3.

Couple 1 continue in the same manner down to the bottom of the set, making arches and passing under alternately.

Couple 2 and each succeeding couple in turn, on reaching the top of the set, turn about, face down the hall, form an arch and repeat the movement down the set as described for couple 1.

When couple 1 reach the bottom of the set, they turn about, pass under the arch of couple 2 and continue back up the set in the same manner, making arches and passing under, until they reach their original places. Each succeeding couple arriving at the bottom of the set proceed up to place again in the same manner as described for couple 1.

As each couple reach their places they stand idle until all have concluded the 'waves', having faced their partners in lines.

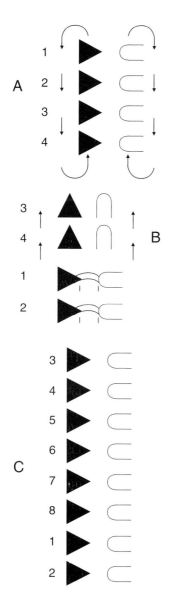

(G) Cast Off

Couple 1 release hands.

Cast off (lady to the right and gent to the left) and march down the set followed by the other dancers who have marched to couple 1's position and cast off in the same manner.

When they reach the bottom, couples 1 and 2 take both hands uncrossed and raise them to form an arch. Couple 3 take inside hands and pass under the arch and up to the top of the set, followed by the other dancers.

When all have passed under, they form again in two lines, partners facing each other, but couples 1 and 2 remain at the bottom of the set.

The dance is now repeated with couple 3 now leading. On the next repeat, when couple 5 are the leading pair, all will be dancing movements (B) and (C) again.

The Rakes Of Mallow – Progressive Long Dance

This dance was arranged by the late Father Lorcan Ó Muireadhaigh during a Céilithe in the Irish College,
Omeath.

Music – Reel of the same name, 'The Rakes of Mallow', or any reel.

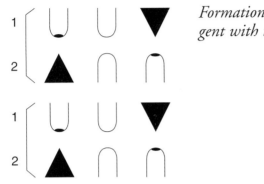

Formation – Three face three. The trios consist of a gent with two ladies on his right.

Steps – Promenade Step, Swing, Threes.

Dance Movements

A. Advance and Retire	= 8 Bars
B. Swing with Opposite Lady	= 8 Bars
C. Swing with Lady on Right	= 8 Bars
D. Link arms in Centre	= 8 Bars
E. Swing Out	= 8 Bars

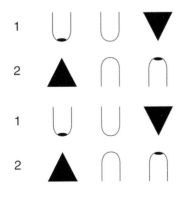

(A) Advance and Retire
The two trios in each set, holding hands, advance towards each other with Promenade Step and retire. Repeat the same movement.

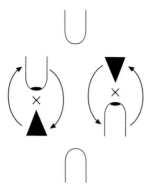

(B) Swing with Opposite Lady

The gents and the ladies opposite then take hands crossed and swing eight Threes in place; centre ladies remain stationary.

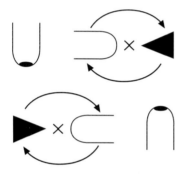

(C) Swing with Lady on Right

The gents and ladies on their right take hands crossed and swing eight Threes in place, other ladies remain stationary.

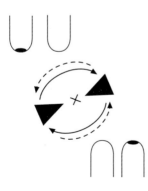

(D) Link Arms in Centre

The gents link right arms in centre and with Promenade Step dance round clockwise.

Turn and link left arms, dancing anti-clockwise, finishing up between two partners.

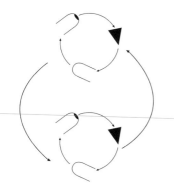

(E) Swing Out
Each gent and his two partners form a ring of three. Each ring (revolving clockwise) swings out and round, to meet the trio in the next set who had been facing them, and line up as at the beginning of the dance, to recommence – ladies having exchanged places.

The Walls of Limerick – Progressive Long Dance
A very popular and easy dance from Limerick in the south of Ireland.

Music – Reels.

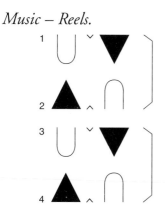

Formation – Two face two. Line up in couples, lady on gent's right, each set of two couples facing each other.

Steps – Promenade Step, Side Step, Threes.

Dance Movements		
	A. Advance and Retire	= 8 Bars
	B. Half Right and Left	= 8 Bars
	C. Dance with Opposite	= 8 Bars
	D. Dance Around	= 8 Bars

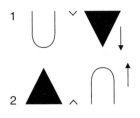

(A) Advance and Retire

Gent takes partner's left hand in his right, both advance to meet the opposite couple and retire to place.
Repeat this movement once.

(B) Half Right and Left

Ladies exchange places with each other by side stepping, starting with their left foot across to opposite lady's position, passing each other face to face, and finishing with two Short Threes.

Gents now exchange places by side stepping to their right commencing with their right foot to opposite gent's place passing face to face and ending with two Short Threes.

(C) Dance with Opposite

Gents takes right hand of opposite lady, both side step to gent's left away from the centre, finishing with two Short Threes.

They then side step back to place, finishing with two Short Threes.

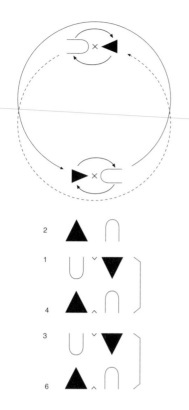

(D) Dance Around

Gent takes own partner's crossed hands, both dance a complete circle around opposite couple, finishing up to face in the opposite direction.

(Note: This movement is more commonly danced as a swing at dances today.)

Repeat the movements with the next couple and with each succeeding couple as you progress until the music stops.

The Siege of Ennis – Progressive Long Dance

A very popular dance on social occasions from Ennis, County Clare, in the west of Ireland.

Music – Jig.

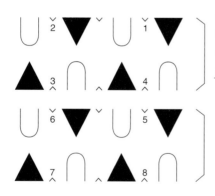

Formation – Dancers line up in fours, two couples in each line. Each set of two couples stands facing another set of two couples, each gent on his partner's left.

Dance Movements

A. Advance and Retire	= 8 Bars
B. Side Step	= 8 Bars
C. Hands Across	= 8 Bars
D. Advance, Retire and Pass Through	= 8 Bars

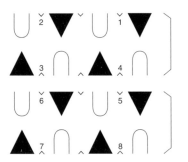

(A) Advance and Retire
Each set of four dancers take hands and advance to
opposite four; they retire and advance and retire again.

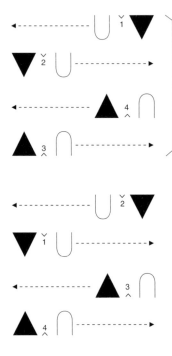

(B) Side Step
The couple on the left of each line of four side step to
the right behind, ending with Rise and Grind, while
couple on right of each line of four side step to left
passing in front, ending with the Rise and Grind.
All now side step back to place.
The couple now in the right-hand side position side step
to the left and in front and the couple in the left position
side step to the right and behind.
All end with the Rise and Grind.

(C) Hands Across

The two ladies and two gents facing each other in the centre give right hands across and dance four Promenade Steps around clockwise.

They then release hands, turn and give left hands across into centre and dance anti-clockwise back to place.

At the same time the gent on the left of each line of four takes right hand of the lady opposite him, both dance around clockwise.

They then release hands, turn and take left hands and dance anti-clockwise back to place.

(Note: This movement is often danced at social dances as a swing, by all dancers taking the opposite dancer and swinging in place for 8 bars.

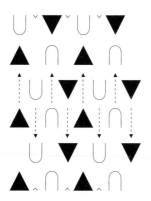

(D) Advance, Retire and Pass Through

Advance and retire once as explained in movement (A). All advance again.

Each set of four facing the music raise hands allowing opposite four to pass under, one dancer under each arch, outer gents passing on the outside, all advancing so as to meet oncoming set of four dancers.

Repeat movements with each successive set.

The Four-Hand Reel

Dance originated in County Cork approximately 1898. Very popular at social gatherings, house dances and ceilis.

Music – Reel.

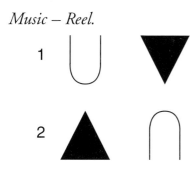

Formation – Two face two, lady on gent's right.

Steps – Promenade Step, Side Step, Sevens and Threes.

Dance Movements		
	A. Lead Around	= 16 Bars
	B. The Square	= 16 Bars
	C. Four Sevens	= 8 Bars
	D. Hands Across	= 8 Bars
	E. Down the Centre	= 8 Bars
	F. Right and Left Chain	= 8 Bars
	G. First Figure	= 32 Bars
	H. Second Figure	= 16 Bars
	I. Finish	= 16 Bars

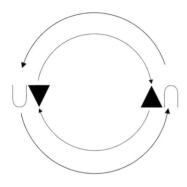

(A) Lead Around

Gent holding lady's left hand in his right hand, half-right turn and lead around a complete circle anti-clockwise dancing eight Promenade Steps; they release hands, about turn inwards, gent takes partner's right hand in his left and both dance back clockwise eight Promenade Steps to place.

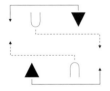

The Body

(B) The Square

Dancers dance four Sevens and four Threes in a square. Gents side step to the right dancing Sevens and two Short Threes on the corners passing behind their partners.

Ladies side step to the left dancing Sevens and two Short Threes on the corners, passing in front of their partners.

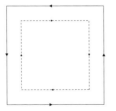

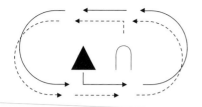

(C) Four Sevens

The dancers are now back in their original positions.
The gents side step to their right behind their partner
and into partner's position.

At the same time the lady side steps to the left and in
front of her partner.

They then side step back to place – this time the gent is
side stepping to the left and in front, and the lady side
steps to the right and behind.

There are no Short Threes danced in this movement, just
the Side Step.

(D) Hands Across

All give right hands across in the centre and dance
around clockwise with four Promenade Steps.

They then release hands, turn and give left hands into
centre and dance four Promenade Steps anti-clockwise
back to place.

(E) Down the Centre

Leading couple turn to face each other, take right hands
and side step through the centre to the place occupied by
the opposite couple. At the same time the opposite
couple turn to face each other and side step to the top
couple's position dancing separately on the outside.
Leading couple half-turn in place, release hands while
opposite couple take right hands and half-turn. Opposite
couple side step back to place through the centre, while
leading couple side step separately up the outside.

Each couple take hands and half-turn to original position.

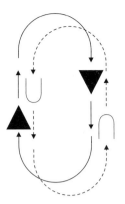

(F) Right and Left Chain

Gent gives right hand to opposite lady.

Both move forward in a semi-circle, gents clockwise and ladies anti-clockwise.

Continue to meet partner with left hand, then opposite lady with right hand, and on to own partner with left hand.

Finish in position, having completed the circular chain.

The Body ends

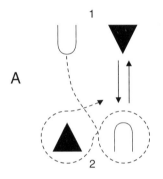

(G) First Figure – Figure of Eight and Rings of Three

(a) Leading couple take inside hands and advance to opposite couple and release hands.

Leading gent retires to place and stands in position, while his partner dances 'The Figure of Eight' by passing between opposite couple, going first round the lady to the left and then back in between the couple and round the opposite gent.

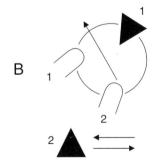

(b) The two ladies now advance to leading gent and take hands in a 'Ring of Three'. Leading couple and opposite lady in the 'Ring of Three' side step to the right (anti-clockwise) ending with two Short Threes, and then side step to the left (clockwise).

At the same time the opposite gent side steps to the right, ending with two Short Threes and then side steps back to place.

Leading couple now arch arms and allow the opposite lady to pass under to the leading lady's original position, then advance and take in the opposite gent and form a 'Ring of Three'.

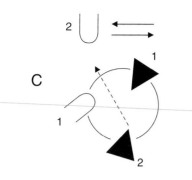

C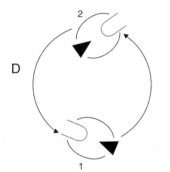

(c) Leading couple and opposite gent now side step in a ring to the left (clockwise) ending with two Threes and then side step back.

Meanwhile opposite lady side steps to the left, ending with two Short Threes and then side steps back to the right.

Leading couple arch arms and allow opposite gent to pass under to his partner.

D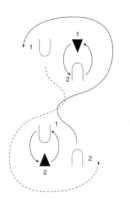

(d) Both couples then swing half-round, anti-clockwise to original places.

The opposite couple now perform the Figure.

Repeat the Body.

(H) The Second Figure – Ladies Chain

Ladies advance, giving right hand to each other in the centre and continue on to the opposite gent, giving them their left hand while both turn anti-clockwise in place.

The ladies return to their own partner giving them their right hand.

They make a full turn in place.

Both couples now dance a complete circle around each other (dance around).

Repeat the Body.

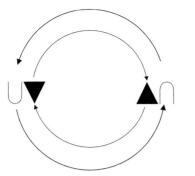

(I) Finish (Lead Around)
Repeat (A).

The Humours of Bandon

Four-Hand Dance from Bandon in County Cork, in the south of Ireland.

Music – Danced to the tune of the same name; the Body is always danced to the second part of the tune and the Figures to the first.

Formation – A set of two couples facing each other.

Steps – Promenade Step, Side Step, Rising Step.

Dance Movements		
	A. Lead Around	= 16 Bars
	B. Sides	= 8 Bars
	C. Half-Right and Left	= 8 Bars
	D. Sides	= 8 Bars
	E. Half-Right and Left	= 8 Bars
	F. First Figure	= 16 Bars
	G. Second Figure	= 16 Bars
	H. Third Figure	= 16 Bars
	I. Finish	= 16 Bars

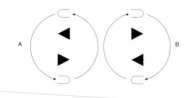

(A) Lead Around

Dancers half-right turn and Lead Around with eight
Promenade Steps anti-clockwise in a complete circle.
Release hands, about turn inwards.
Gent takes partner's right hand in his left and both dance
clockwise back to place.

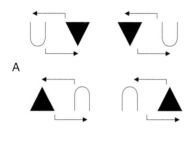

The Body

(B) Sides

Gents side step to right behind partners while ladies side
step in front.
All end with Rising Step.
Side step back to place, gents in front, ending with
Rising Step.

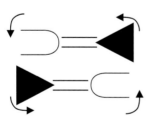

(C) Half-Right and Left

Partners take both hands, turn once in place.
Release hands, gents and ladies cross to opposite position,
gents crossing on the outside, ladies passing between
opposite gent and lady.

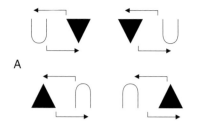

A

(D) Sides

Gents side step to right behind partners while ladies side step in front.

All end with Rising Step.

Side step back to place, gents in front ending with Rising Step.

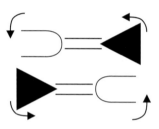

(E) Half-Right and Left

Partners take both hands, turn once in place.

Release hands, gents and ladies cross to opposite position, gents crossing on the outside, ladies passing between opposite gent and lady.

The Body ends

(F) First Figure – Advance Through Centre

Leading gent takes his partner's left hand in his right, both advance towards opposite couple; pass between and beyond them.

Release hands, turn about and return to opposite couple, lady's right hand in gent's left, release hands.

Lady takes opposite gent's left hand in her left hand.

Leading gent takes opposite lady's right hand in his right.

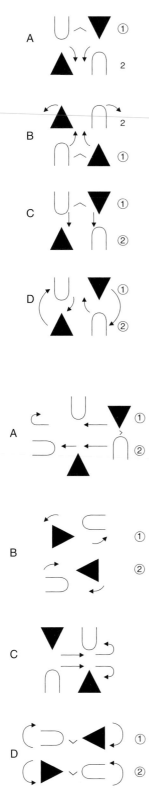

A

All turn once in place, leading gent takes his partner's right hand in his left and they lead back to place. Release hands and turn about, advance again, lady's left hand in gent's right, release hands.

Gent gives left hand to opposite lady; leading lady gives right hand to opposite gent.

B

All turn once in place, release hands.

Leading couple dance back to place and turn once in place.

C

Repeat the Body.

Opposite couple dance the first Figure.

Repeat the Body.

D

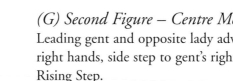

(G) Second Figure – Centre Meet

A

Leading gent and opposite lady advance to meet, take right hands, side step to gent's right, ending with the Rising Step.

Lady now takes own partner's right hand in her right. Gent takes own partner's hand, left hand in his left and all turn in place.

B

Same gent and lady meet again in centre and take left hands and side step to gent's left, ending with the Rising Step.

Release hands, lady gives left hand to own partner's left, gent gives right hand to his partner's right.

They all turn in place.

C

Repeat the Body.

Opposite couple repeat the second Figure.

D

Repeat the Body.

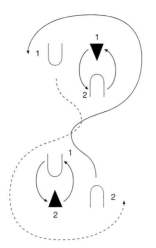

(H) Third Figure – Ladies Chain

Ladies advance to opposite lady and give right hands in centre, continue to opposite gent giving left hand.

Both turn in place, and ladies return to own partner and give right hand.

Both make a full turn in place.

Both couples take both hands crossed and dance a complete circle (anti-clockwise) around each other and back to place.

Repeat the Body.

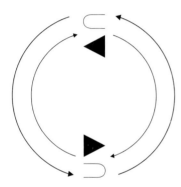

(I) Finish – Lead Around

Dancers half-right turn and lead around with eight Promenade Steps anti-clockwise in a complete circle. Release hands, about turn inwards, gent takes partner's right hand in his left and both dance clockwise back to place.

The Harvest-Time Jig – Progressive Long Dance

Music – Jig time.

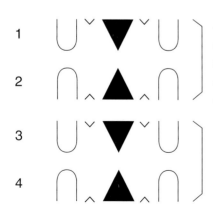

Formation – Three dancers face three dancers in a line. Each gent has two lady partners. Gent stands in the middle of the two ladies. The gent holds the left hand of the lady on his right and the right hand of the lady on his left.

Steps – Promenade Step, Side Step, Rising Step, Sink and Grind.

Dance Movements

A. Advance and Retire	= 8 Bars
B. Side Step	= 8 Bars
C. Right Hands Across	= 8 Bars
D. Side Step	= 8 Bars
E. Left Hands Across	= 8 Bars
F. Step and Turn	= 16 Bars
G. Advance, Retire and Pass Through	= 8 Bars

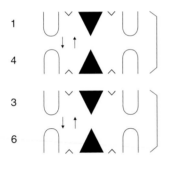

A) Advance and Retire
All dancers advance and retire twice.

(B) Side Step
Each set of three dancers side step to the right, ending with the Rising Step on their right foot.
They then side step back to the left, ending with the Rising Step on their left foot.

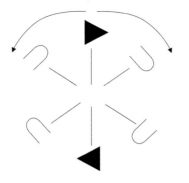

(C) Right Hands Across

All give right hands across in the centre and dance around clockwise with four Promenade Steps.

They then release hands, turn and give left hands into centre and dance four Promenade Steps anti-clockwise back to place.

(D) Side Step

Each set of three dancers side step to the left and end with the Rising Step on their left foot.

They then side step back to the right and end with Rising Step on their right foot.

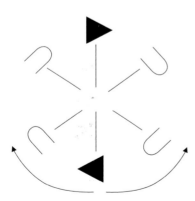

(E) Left Hands Across

All give left hands across in the centre and dance around anti-clockwise with four Promenade Steps.

They then release hands, turn and give right hands into centre and dance four Promenade Steps clockwise back to place.

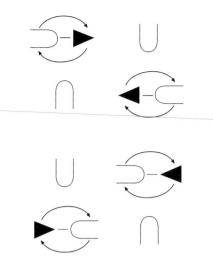

F) Step and Turn

Gent turns towards right-hand partner.

Both dance Sink and Grind twice on the right foot.

Gent then takes lady's right hand and dances around her to his place.

Gent then dances the Sink and Grind twice with his left-hand partner, giving her his left hand and dancing around her to return to his place.

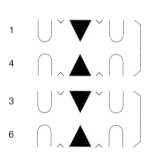

(G) Advance, Retire and Pass Through

All advance and retire once, then release hands and pass through, opposite dancers passing right arm to right arm when passing each other.

The new line-up should be 1 facing 4, 3 facing 6, and so on.

Repeat the movements A–G with each successive set.

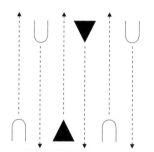

1

4

3

6

The Fairy Reel – Progressive Long Dance

Music – Reels.

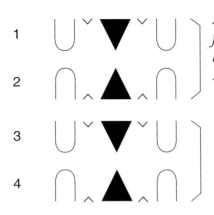

1
2
3
4

Formation – A Six-Hand Dance for two gents and four ladies, forming two trios, the gent having a lady on each side of him. Originally a Square Dance, it is now done as a Progressive Long Dance.

Steps – Promenade Step, Side Step, Threes.

Dance Movements

A. Advance and Retire	= 8 Bars
B. Rings	= 8 Bars
C. Advance and Retire	= 8 Bars
D. Rings	= 8 Bars
E. Slip Sides	=16 Bars
F. Link Arms	=16 Bars
G. The Square	=16 Bars
H. Arches	= 8 Bars
I. Pass Through	= 8 Bars

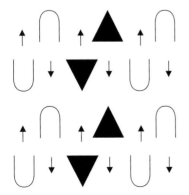

(A) Advance and Retire
Gents take partners' inside hands, and all three advance in line to meet the opposite trio with two Promenade Steps.
The lines now retire to place with two Promenade Steps.
The lines advance and retire once more and on the last two Threes.
All six dancers form into a large ring taking hands.

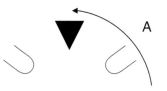

(B) Rings
All side step to the right (anti-clockwise), finishing with two Short Threes, side step back to the left (clockwise), finishing with two Short Threes.

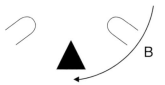

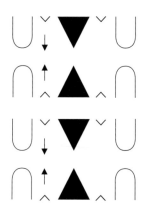

(C) Advance and Retire
Gents take partners' inside hands, and all three advance in line to meet the opposite trio with two Promenade Steps.
The lines now retire to place with two Promenade Steps. The lines advance and retire once more, and on the last two Threes all six dancers form into a large ring taking hands.

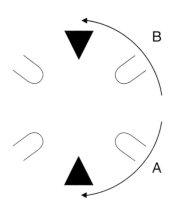

(D) Rings
All side step to the left (clockwise), finishing with two Short Threes, side step back to the right (anti-clockwise), finishing with two Short Threes.
On the last two Threes each gent turns to face lady on his right, who also turns to face him.

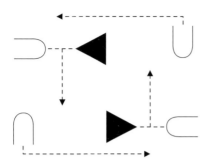

(E) Slip Sides

The gent and the lady on his right side, who are now facing each other, take right hands and dance a Side Step and two Short Threes to gent's left, and then side step right back to places ending with two Short Threes.

On the Threes each gent turns left to face partner on left. While this movement is being danced the free partner side steps to the right, ending with two Short Threes and then side steps to the left back to place, ending with two Short Threes.

On the last Three she turns to face gent.

The gent now side steps to the right with the lady on the left, ending with two Short Threes.

They then side step left back to their positions ending with two Short Threes.

In the meantime the other lady on the right side steps to the left, ending with two Threes, and then to the right back to place, ending with two Threes.

(F) Link Arms

Gents dance in to centre with Promenade Step, and linking right arms, continue round clockwise to complete four bars.

They then turn, link left arms and dance round anti-clockwise a further four bars back to places, finishing up facing partner on the right.

Gent now gives right hand to partner on right and turns once.

Then he passes on to partner on left whom he turns with left arm.

He now turns to lady on right again whom he turns in place with right hand and so back to place.

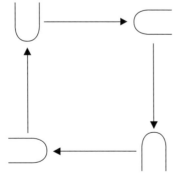

(G) The Square

The four ladies dance a square, the partner on gent's left side steps to the right and behind to the place of the other partner, the partner on the right side steps to the left passing in front.

All end with two Short Threes, turning to face each other on the second Three.

This movement is repeated in the same direction another three times to complete the four sides of a square.

At the same time the gents do a similar Side Step and Threes movement, but in the shape of a diamond. Each gent side steps to right from his position to the centre of the side of the square on his right, and so on until he returns to his original position.

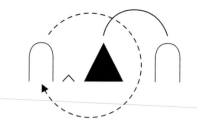

(H) Arches

The gent now takes inside hands with partners, raises right hand to form arch and, passing the partner on left under the arch, he also passes under it.

He now raises his left hand and passes the right-hand partner under the arch, again passing under it himself.

He repeats the first arch and all fall back into place, but continue to hold hands.

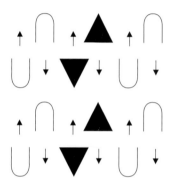

(I) Pass Through

Trios advance and retire with the Promenade Step.

All release hands, advance again, pass through, right arm to right arm, and face a new trio to recommence dance.

The Fairy Reel has several variations. The description above is the one in the Dance Commission Book.

The version most commonly danced at dances has the following changes:

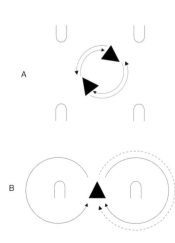

A–E as above. Then:

(F) Gents Centre and Link Arms   Gents Centre and Link Arms

When the gent finishes the Side Step with the partner on his left he is holding her right hand in his right.

He dances around the lady on his left with the Promenade Step and then gives his left hand to his partner on his right. He dances around her and back to his partner on his left, taking her right hand in his right as he dances around her and back to his starting position.

The above movement is the same as a Figure of Eight.

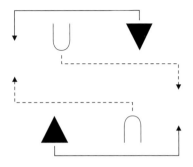

(G) The Square

The gent takes the hand of the lady on his left and they both dance a square side stepping to the right and behind the partner on their right who is side stepping to the left. All end with two Threes, and on the second Three all turn.

They continue the square until they arrive back in their starting position.

(H) is not danced in this variation.

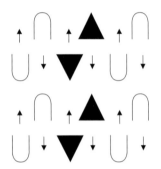

(I) Pass Through

Trios advance and retire with the Promenade Step.

All release hands, advance again, pass through, right arm to right arm, and face a new trio to recommence dance.

The Glencar Reel

Music – Reels.

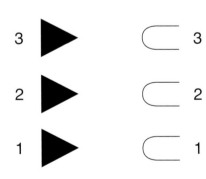

Formation – This is a dance for six people, three gents and three ladies. Line up in two rows, the gents on one side and the ladies on the other, partners facing each other.

Steps – Side Step, Threes, Promenade Step.

Dance Movements

A. Advance and Retire		= 8 Bars
B. Rings		= 8 Bars
C. Side Step Through		= 8 Bars
D. Figure of Eight		= 8 Bars
E. Double Figure of Eight		= 8 Bars
F. The Waves		= 8 Bars
G. Full Chain		= 8 Bars

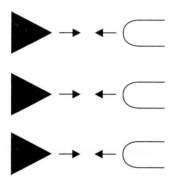

(A) Advance and Retire

Dancers form up in two lines, take hands, advance with two Promenade Steps and retire with two Promenade Steps.

Repeat this movement once.

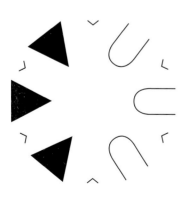

(B) Rings

All dancers take hands to form a ring and side step to the left (clockwise), finishing with two Short Threes.

All side step back to place, falling back into line while dancing the two Threes.

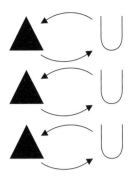

(C) Side Step Through

All dancers turn left and side step right to partners' places (partners passing face to face) and finish with two Short Threes.

All side step back to place, finishing with two Short Threes and turning into original positions.

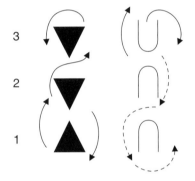

(D) Figure of Eight

With Promenade Step ladies dance the Figure of Eight on their side, while gents dance the Figure of Eight at the same time on their side.

The 1st and 2nd ladies turn right to face the 3rd lady, who faces left.

The 2nd lady commences by dancing around the 3rd lady, passing right shoulder to right shoulder.

The 3rd lady, who has danced forward, passes around the 1st lady, left shoulder to left shoulder.

The 1st lady, advancing, passes around the 2nd lady, passing right shoulder to right shoulder.

The dancers continue until each by these interlacing movements has completed the Figure of Eight.

The 2nd and 3rd gents turn right to face the 1st gent, who turns left.

The Figure of Eight is commenced by the 2nd gent who dances around the 1st gent, passing right shoulder to right and so on until the Figure of Eight is completed.

On the last two bars partners should advance towards each other and join both hands (not crossed), to be ready to start the next movement.

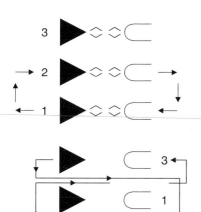

(E) Double Figure of Eight

Couples with hands already joined dance the Figure of Eight by interlacing the 2nd and 3rd couple and turn right to face the 1st couple who turn left.

The Figure of Eight is commenced by the 2nd couple who dance around the 1st couple, passing right shoulders to right shoulders and so on until the Figure is completed.

(F) The Waves

The 1st couple face the other two couples, holding inside hands raised, and the 2nd couple also holding inside hands pass underneath.

The 1st couple in turn bend and pass under the arms of the 3rd couple, now at the top.

The movement is continued until all return to original places.

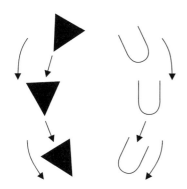

(G) Full Chain

A Ring is again formed, gents turn to move with Promenade Step anti-clockwise, while ladies turn to meet them and move around clockwise.

The 1st gent gives right hand to partner and chains on to meet the next lady, taking her left hand in his left.

The chain movement is continued until all return to their original positions.

The Duke Reel – Round Dance

This dance is said to have been composed by Dick Duke from St Margaret's, north County Dublin, in the mid twentieth century.

Music – Reel.

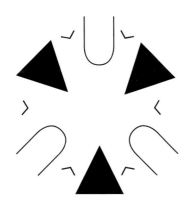

Formation – Three couples stand in a ring holding hands.

Steps – Side Step, Threes, Promenade Step.

Dance Movements		
	A. Rings	= 8 Bars
	B. Sides	= 16 Bars
	C. Link Arms	= 8 Bars
	D. Interlace	= 8 Bars
	E. Advance and Retire	= 8 Bars
	F. First Figure	= 16 Bars
	G. Second Figure	= 16 Bars
	H. Finish	= 8 Bars

(A) Rings

All couples take hands in a circle.

All side step in a ring anti-clockwise finishing with two Short Threes.

Side step back to place clockwise ending with two Short Threes.

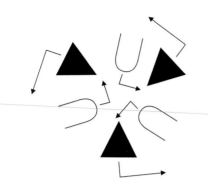

The Body
(B) Sides
Partners side step past each other, gents passing behind, finishing with two Short Threes.
Side step back to place, gents passing in front, all ending with two Short Threes.
Gents do the same movement with the ladies on their left; this time the ladies pass behind when going right, and in front when returning to place.

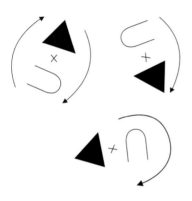

(C) Link Arms
Partners link right arms and dance a full turn clockwise. Each gent now links left arm with lady on left of original position and turns anti-clockwise.
This movement is now repeated, dancers ending in original positions.

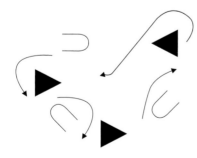

(D) Interlace
Partners face each other and pass with Promenade Step, right shoulder to right shoulder.
They pass the next dancer left shoulder to left shoulder, and the next right shoulder to right, passing alternately on either side as in any chain movement, except that hands are not taken.

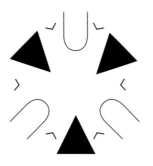

E) Advance and Retire

All join hands in a circle and advance two Promenade Steps towards the centre.

All now retire to place.

All advance once again but on retiring release non-partners' hands and fall into position to be ready for the Figure.

The Body ends

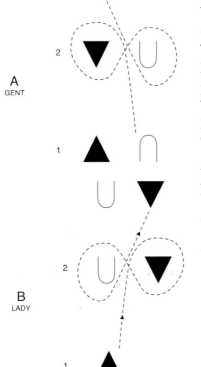

A
GENT

B
LADY

(F) First Figure – Figure of Eight

With Promenade Step couple 1 advance towards couple 2 (couple 3 stand idle).

The lady of couple 1 passes between couple 2 followed by her partner, while the lady makes a Figure of Eight by passing around the lady and then the gent.

The gent of couple 1 passes around the gent and then the lady.

This leaves couple 1 on the inside of couple 2, and they join hands in a ring (8 bars).

All four side step left (clockwise) finishing with two Short Threes (4 bars), and the partners take both hands and swing back into places (4 bars).

The Figure is repeated by couple 2 who pass through and dance with couple 3, while couple 1 stand idle.

Couple 3 repeat the Figure by passing through and dancing with couple 1, while couple 2 stand idle.

Repeat the Body.

A

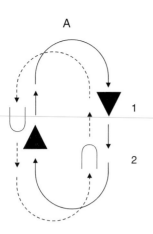

(G) Second Figure – Right and Left Chain

Gents of couples 1 and 2 give right hand to opposite ladies.

Both move forward in a semi-circle, gents clockwise and ladies anti-clockwise, and continue to meet partner with left hand, then opposite lady with right hand, and on to own partner with left hand.

Finish in position having completed the circular chain (8 bars).

Both couples now dance a complete circle around each other (8 bars).

The Figure is now performed by couples 2 and 3 and then by couples 3 and 1.

Repeat the Body.

B

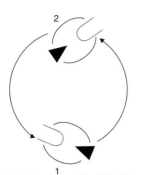

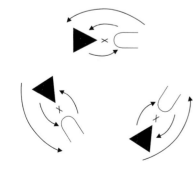

(H) Finish

Partners hold hands crossed and swing around in couples anti-clockwise back to place.

The Cross Reel

Music – Reels.

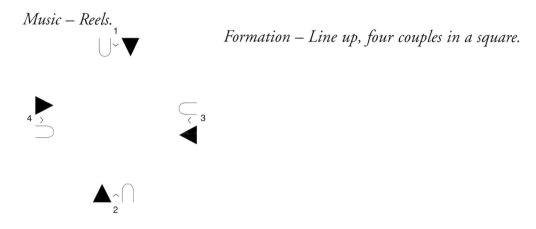

Formation – Line up, four couples in a square.

Steps – Promenade Step, Side Step, Threes, Sevens.

Dance Movements		
	A. Lead Around	= 16 Bars
	B. Extended Sides	= 16 Bars
	C. Full Chain	= 16 Bars
	D. Gentlemen Interlace	= 16 Bars
	E. Back to Back	= 8 Bars
	F. Exchange Places	= 8 Bars
	G. First Figure	= 32 Bars
	H. Second Figure	= 32 Bars
	I. Finish	= 40 Bars

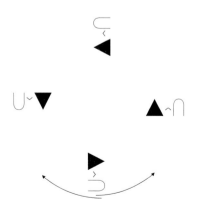

(A) Lead Around
Dancers take hands, gent holds lady's left in his right, half-right turn and dance anti-clockwise around with eight Promenade Steps in a complete circle.
They then release hands, about turn inwards.
Gent takes partner's right hand in his left.
All then dance eight Promenade Steps clockwise back to their starting position.

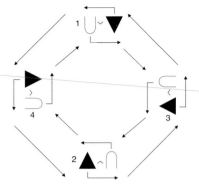

The Body
(B) Extended Sides

Gents side step to right, finish with two Threes, repeat to right again.

Give right hand to lady in the right position, dance a full turn and chain back to their partner, left hand to next lady and right hand to partner and turn into place.

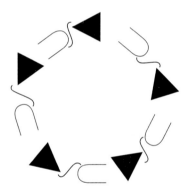

(C) Full Chain

Partners face each other and take right hands (ladies turn left, gents to the right) and start to chain, giving left hand to the next lady and gent.

Continue on until they arrive back in home position.

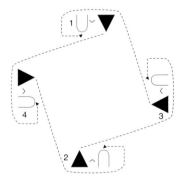

(D) Gentlemen Interlace

Gents dance to right in front of partner, behind lady on right, and into a position facing the lady on the right. Gents give lady left hand, make a full turn, give right hand across into centre, and left hand to the lady before their partner.

Make a full turn and back to partner with right hand and turn with partner into place.

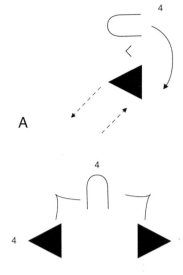

(E) Back to Back

Gent takes partner's right hand and dances forward, to the right for tops and left for sides.

The gent gives his left hand to the lady of side couple, side gent gives left hand to lady of top couple.

All dance two Threes while holding hands.

Gent releases partner's hand and dances a full turn with the other lady, still holding her left hand.

Gent now releases his left hand and dances back to his partner, giving her his right hand and turning into place.

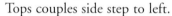

(F) Exchange Places

Tops couples side step to left.

Side couples side step to the right. Sevens and no Threes.

In the new position couples change Side Step with their own partner. No Threes.

Holding this position (gents in ladies' position) all side step back to home position. No Threes.

All side step with partner in home position, gents to left, ladies to right. No Threes.

The Body ends

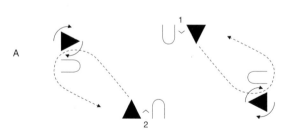

(G) First Figure – Figures of Eight and Ring

Top gents dance in between the side couples on their left with Promenade Step and make a Figure of Eight, passing through the couple, and then around the gent, and in between the couple again, around the lady and back to home position.

When the gent returns to place, all take

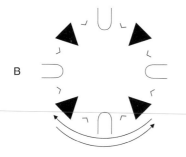

hands and side step right and dance two Threes, side step back to place and dance two Short Threes.

Sides now perform the Figure, the gents dancing to the right.

Repeat the Body.

(H) Second Figure – Circle Around and Hands Across

Top couples advance and dance back to back.

Top couples now give right hand into centre and dance full round.

The two couples now dance around each other in an anti-clockwise direction, revolving clockwise back to place.

Sides repeat the Figure.

(I) Finish

All dancers join hands in the circle, forearms bent sharply upwards, elbows held in to the sides.

Advance to centre, retire, advance again and retire.

All side step right (anti-clockwise) and finish with two Short Threes.

Side step back to left (clockwise) ending with two Short Threes.

Advance and retire twice as before.

All side step left (clockwise) ending with two Short Threes and side step back to the right (anti-clockwise), ending with two Short Threes.

Each couple take hands, swing around to the right and finish off.

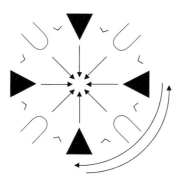

The Sweets of May

This is an old Northern Ireland dance from Armagh.

Music – Tune of the same name in double jig time.
Formation – Four couples join hands in a circle.

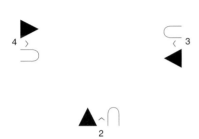

Steps – Promenade Step, Side Step, Dance Around.

Dance Movements		
A. First Figure	=	16 Bars
B. Cross Over and Back	=	8 Bars
C. Advance and Retire	=	8 Bars
D. Ringing the Bells	=	16 Bars
E. Second Figure	=	16 Bars
F. Third Figure	=	16 Bars
G. Fourth Figure	=	16 Bars
H. Rings	=	16 Bars

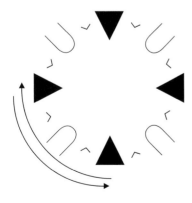

(A) First Figure – Rings

All dancers join hands in a Ring of Eight and side step to the left clockwise, finishing with two Short Threes. Side step to the right anti-clockwise, finishing with two Short Threes.

The side step movement is then repeated, this time side step to the right (anti-clockwise), ending with two Short Threes, and then all side step to the left (clockwise) ending with two Short Threes. While doing the last two Threes all couples, breaking the ring, fall back to their original places, partners retaining inside hands.

The Body

(B) Cross Over and Back

Top couples, holding inside hands, exchange places with Promenade Step, passing across, gents left shoulder to left shoulder.

While top couples are exchanging places, side couples dance two Threes in place.

Side couples exchange place in like manner, while top couples dance two Threes.

Tops dance back to their original positions with the Promenade Step while sides dance two Short Threes.

Sides now dance back to their original positions while tops dance two Short Threes.

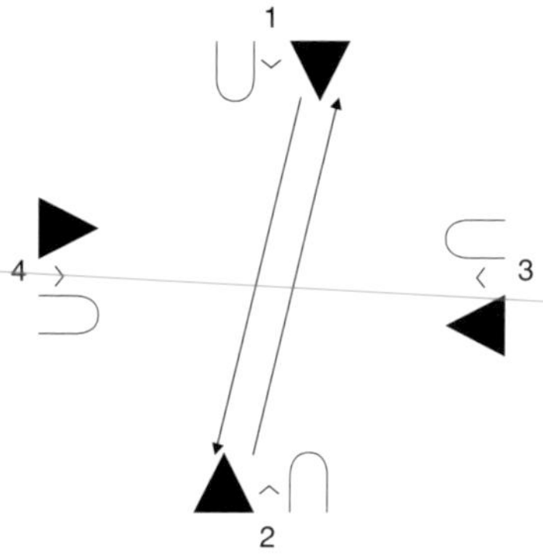

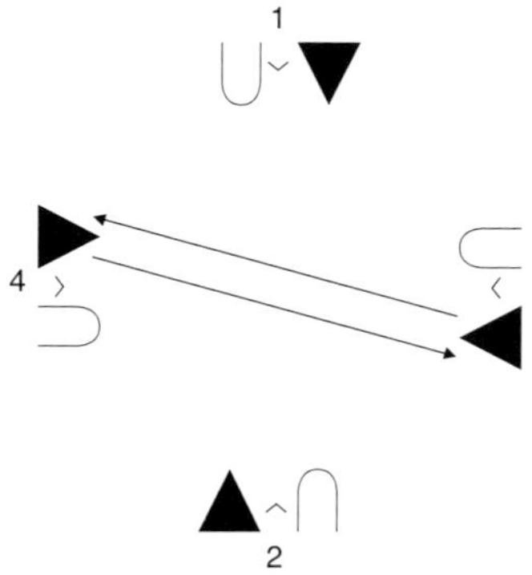

(C) Advance and Retire

Top couples, still holding hands, advance to meet in centre, while side couples mark time with two Threes.

Sides advance to centre while tops retire.

Tops advance while sides retire.

Tops retire while sides mark time.

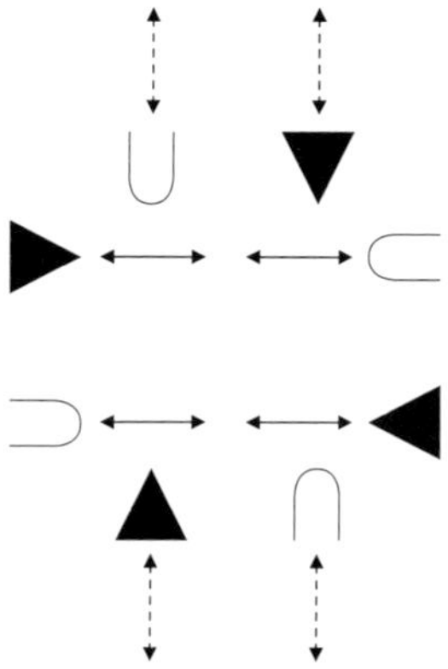

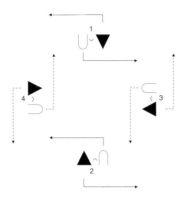

(D) Ringing the Bells

All dancers bend and beat left hand on left knee and right hand on right knee four times; then clap hands in front of forehead twice.

Repeat movement from the beginning.

Partners side step past each other, the gents passing behind to the right and at the same time ladies passing to the left and in front.

All dance two Threes in new places.

This movement is now repeated, but this time gents side step to the left and in front, and ladies side step to the right behind ending with two Short Threes.

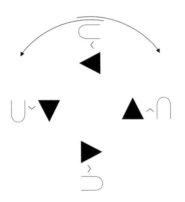

The Body ends

(E) Second Figure – Lead Around

Partners hold inside hands, and dance around a complete circle with eight Promenade Steps anti-clockwise; release hands, about turn inwards, take inside hands.

Gent holds lady's right hand in his left.

All dance eight Promenade Steps clockwise back to original positions.

Repeat the Body.

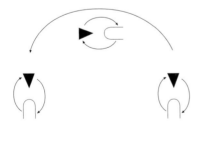

(F) Third Figure – See-Saw

All couples face their partners, take uncrossed hands, and dance around (revolving clockwise) in an anti-clockwise direction until they reach their starting position. Couples now return clockwise, revolving in an anti-clockwise direction until they return to their original position.

Repeat the Body.

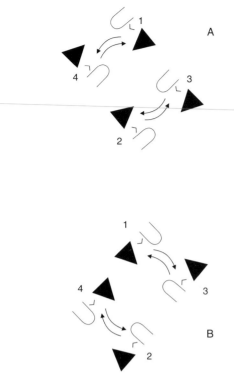

(G) Fourth Figure – Sides Under Arms

Partners take inside hands.

Top couples hold up hands to form an arch, and dance with Promenade Step to their right into side couples' position.

At the same time side couples dance to their left and under the arch of the top couples.

All release hands and face about.

All take inside hands again and dance back to places, this time sides making arches and tops passing underneath.

This whole movement is now repeated.

Top couples now make an arch and dance to the left to the position of the side couple.

At the same time side couples dance to their right to the position of the top couple and under the arch of the top couples.

All release hands and face about.

All take inside hands again and dance back to places.

This time side couples make the arches and top couples dance under back to original positions.

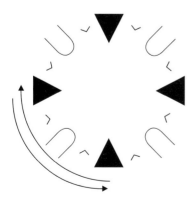

Repeat the Body.

(H) Rings

All dancers join hands in a Ring of Eight and side step to the left clockwise, finishing with two Short Threes, side step to the right anti-clockwise, finishing with two Short Threes. The Side Step movement is then repeated, this time side stepping to the right moving anti-clockwise, ending with two Short Threes and then all side step to the left clockwise ending with two Short Threes.

While doing the last two Threes, all couples, breaking the ring, fall back to their original places, partners retaining inside hands.

Eight-Hand Reel

Music – Reels.

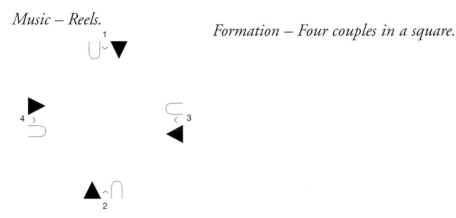

Formation – Four couples in a square.

Steps – Promenade Step, Side Step, Threes.

Dance Movements		
	A. Lead Around	= 16 Bars
	B. Extended Sides	= 16 Bars
	C. Skip Across	= 32 Bars
	D. Return Chain	= 16 Bars
	E. Back to Back	= 16 Bars
	F. First Figure	= 16 Bars
	G. Second Figure	= 16 Bars
	H. Finish	= 40 Bars

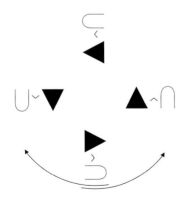

(A) Lead Around
Gent holds lady's left hand in his right hand, half-right turn and dance anti-clockwise around with eight Promenade Steps in a complete circle.
They then release hands, about turn inwards, gent takes partner's right hand in his left.
They all then dance eight Promenade Steps clockwise back to their starting position.

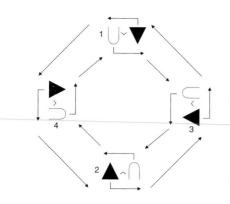

The Body

(B) Extended Sides

Gents side step to the right behind partners, ladies side step to the left in front, finishing with two Short Threes. All again side step on in the same direction as before, and end with two Short Threes.

Each gent takes right hand of lady next to him on his right, both make full turn.

All now chain back as they have come to meet partners with right hand in starting position; turn once in position.

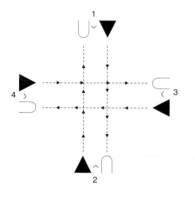

(C) Skip Across

Top gents now exchange places by side stepping, ending with two Short Threes.

Side gents exchange places with the Side Step ending with two Short Threes.

When crossing, gents face each other right arm to right arm, turn lady with right hand, and pass on to lady on left of original position, give left hand and turn in place.

Top gents again exchange places by side stepping as before ending with two Short Threes.

Side gents now exchange places with the Side Step ending with two Short Threes.

Gents turn the ladies with their left hand and dance on to their partner with right hand in original position and turn in place.

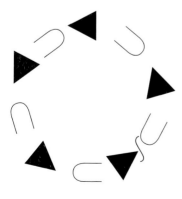

(D) Return Chain

Gents are now in original position, holding partner's right hand in own right.

Couples face each other and start to chain; gents give left hand to lady on right, ladies give left hand to gents on left.

All chain around giving right and left hand alternately until meeting own partner again with right hand at opposite side of the circle (half-way round).

Turn right around partner and chain back to original position, meeting partner with right hand and turning in place.

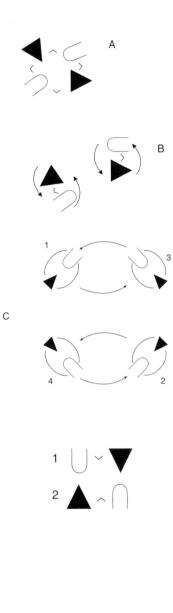

E) Back to Back

Gent, holding partner's right hand, side steps towards the left of contrary lady, while partner dances towards the left of contrary (couple on right of top couple) gent.

Gent then takes left hand of contrary lady while partner takes left hand of contrary gent. The four dancers now form a circle, gents being back to back, ladies facing each other.

All dance two Short Threes.

Gent releases partner's right hand, turns around contrary lady and returns to own partner, passing other gent right arm to right.

Partners take both hands and dance around couple opposite to contrary couple (couple on the left side of top couple) and back to place.

The Body ends

(F) First Figure – Advance and Retire

Leading and opposite tops advance with two Promenade Steps and retire with two Promenade Steps.

They repeat this movement once again.

Both couples then dance complete circle around each other anti-clockwise back to starting position.

Leading and opposite sides now dance the Figure as above.

When both tops and sides have performed the Figure, repeat the Body.

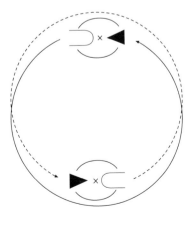

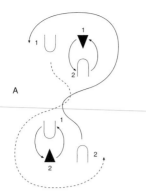

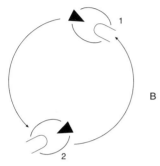

(G) Second Figure – Ladies Chain

Ladies advance towards opposite lady and give right hands in centre; continue to opposite gent giving left hand.

Both turn in place, and ladies return to own partner, both making full turn in place.

Both couples dance complete circle around each other.

Repeat the Body.

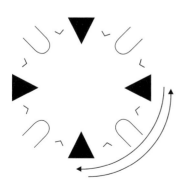

(H) Finish

All dancers join hands in the circle, forearms bent sharply upwards, elbows held in to the sides; advance to centre, retire, advance again and retire.

All side step right (anti-clockwise) and finish with two Short Threes, side step back to left (clockwise) ending with two Short Threes.

Advance and retire twice as before.

All side step left (clockwise) ending with two Short Threes, and side step back to the right (anti-clockwise) ending with two Short Threes.

Each couple take hands and swing around to the right and finish off.

High Caul Cap

This very popular dance, said to have originated in County Kerry in the south of Ireland, was first written down between 1897–1902 from a description given by Professor Patrick D. Reidy, a dancing master from Castleisland, who was Professor of Irish Dancing to the London branch of the Gaelic League.

Music – Reels.

Formation – Four couples in a circle.

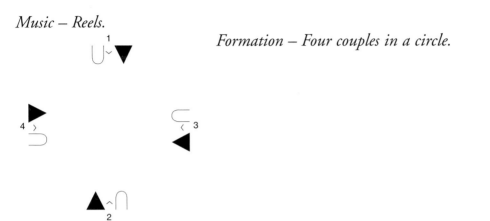

Steps – Promenade Step, Side Step, Threes, Swing.

Dance Movements		
	A. Lead Around	= 16 Bars.
	B. Sides	= 16 Bars
	C. Double Quarter Chain	= 16 Bars
	D. Ladies Interlace	= 16 Bars
	E. Gents Interlace	= 16 Bars
	F. Stamp and Clap	= 16 Bars
	G. First Figure	= 16 Bars
	H. Second Figure	= 24 Bars
	I. Third Figure	= 16 Bars
	J. Finish	= 40 Bars

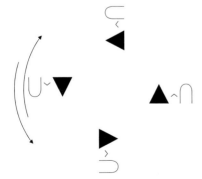

(A) Lead Around

Dancers take hands.

Gent holds lady's left in his right, half-right turn and dance anti-clockwise around with eight Promenade Steps in a complete circle.

They then release hands, about turn inwards.

Gent takes partner's right hand in his left.

They all then dance eight Promenade Steps clockwise back to their starting position.

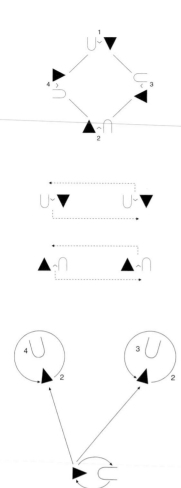

The Body
(B) Sides
Leading and opposite tops side step to the right, while leading and opposite sides side step to the left, all partners holding hands.

All finish with two Short Threes. The position now is that leading and opposite tops have exchanged positions with couple on right.

Now all continue to side step on to next position, finishing with two Short Threes, the dancers now being in the position exactly opposite their starting position. All side step on to the next position, with two Short Threes, and side step on to place, ending with two Short Threes.

(C) Double Quarter Chain
Gent takes partner's right hand in right hand and both turn once in place.

Gent chains with left hand to lady on left, both turn in place, chains back to own partner with right hand, turning in place.

Continue the chain with left hand to lady on right, both turn once in place, chain back to own partner with right hand, both turn once in place.

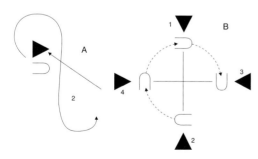

(D) Ladies Interlace
Each lady dances in front of her own partner towards gent on left, passes behind and around in front of him, dances back towards own partner, and behind him to original position. Gents meanwhile remain in position.

Ladies now give right hand across in the centre, dance around to the left (clockwise), drop hands, give left hand to gent on right of lady's original position, both turn once in place, chain on to own partner with right hand and turn into place.

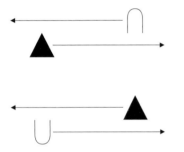

(E) Gents Interlace

Each gent now dances in front of own partner towards lady on right, passes behind and around in front of her, dances back towards own partner and behind her to original position.

Gents give right hand across in centre, dance around to left (clockwise), drop hands, give left hand to lady on right of gent's original position.

Both turn once in place, chain on to own partner with right hand and turn in place.

(F) Stamp and Clap

All stamp right foot twice to one bar, and clap hands three times to second bar.

Repeat this movement once more.

Partners change places by side stepping, gent to the right and behind lady to the left and in front, ending with two Short Threes.

All stamp right foot twice to one bar, and clap hands three times to second bar.

Repeat this movement once more.

Side step back to place, gent to the left and in front, lady to the right and behind, ending with two Short Threes.

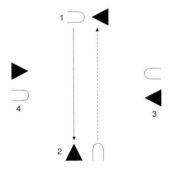

The Body ends

(G) First Figure

Leading tops turn to face each other, take right hands and side step to the gent's left and lady's right up the middle of the set towards opposite couple, ending with two Short Threes.

They now side step back to their place ending with two Short Threes.

Both still holding hands turn once in place and release hands.

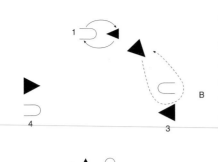

The gent now dances between the couple on his left around the lady and back to place.

At the same time his partner dances between the couple on her right around the gent and back to place.

Gent dances around lady on left and back, while lady dances around gent on right and back.

Both take hands and turn into place.

Opposite tops, leading sides and opposite sides then perform the Figure in that order.

Repeat the Body.

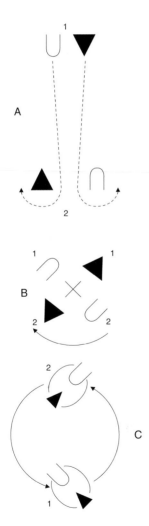

(H) Second Figure – Circle and Cross

Leading tops take hands and with the Promenade Step advance to opposite couple who have their hands by their sides; pass through, lady passing around opposite gent, gent passing around opposite lady.

All four give right hands across and dance around clockwise; release hands, leading tops dancing back to place, opposite tops turning once into position.

Gents advance, passing right arm to right, to opposite lady; take left hand and dance around her.

Release hands, dance back to place, take own partner's right hand and turn in place.

Both couples dance a circle to the right (anti-clockwise) around each other and back to place.

Opposite tops, leading sides and opposite sides now perform the Figure in that order.

Repeat the Body.

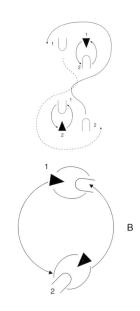

(I) Third Figure – Ladies Chain

Ladies advance to opposite lady and give right hands in centre, continue to opposite gent giving left hand, both turn in place, and ladies return to own partner and give right hand.

Both make a full turn in place.

Both couples take both hands crossed and dance a complete circle (anti-clockwise) around each other and back to place.

The movement is now danced by side couples.

On completion of the Figure repeat the Body.

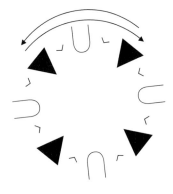

(J) Finish

All dancers join hands in the circle, forearms bent sharply upwards, elbows held in to the sides.

Advance to centre, retire, advance again and retire.

All side step to the right (anti-clockwise) and finish with two Short Threes, side step back ending with two Short Threes.

Advance and retire twice as before.

All side step to the left (clockwise) and back.

Each couple take hands and swing around to the right and finish off.

Eight-Hand Jig

One of the more difficult Eight-Hand Dances. Very popular as a competition dance and also as a social dance. Said to have been originally collected in the region of Kerry in the south of Ireland.

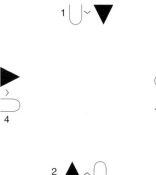

Formation – There are four couples in the set. Couple 1 are leading tops. Couple 2 are opposite tops. Couple 3 are leading sides. Couple 4 are opposite sides.

Steps – Side Step, Promenade Step, Rising Step, Rise and Grind.

Dance Movements		
	A. Lead Around	= 16 Bars
	B. Side Step	= 8 Bars
	C. Skip Across	= 16 Bars
	D. Swing into Line	= 16 Bars
	E. Set All-Round	= 16 Bars
	F. First Figure	= 16 Bars
	G. Second Figure	= 32 Bars
	H. Finish	= 40 Bars

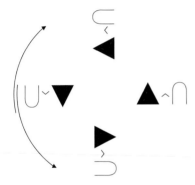

(A) Lead Around

Gent holds lady's left hand in his right, half-right turn and Lead Around a complete circle anti-clockwise dancing eight Promenade Steps.

They release hands and about turn inwards.

Gent takes partner's right hand in his left and both dance back clockwise eight Promenade Steps to place.

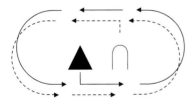

The Body
(B) Side Step

Gent side steps to right behind partner, ending with Rise and Grind, while lady side steps to the left in front of partner.

All side step back to place, gents in front, ladies behind, ending with Rise and Grind.

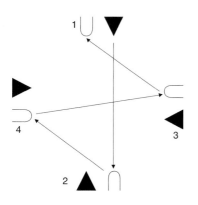

(C) Skip Across

The four gents cross to opposite ladies, tops a fraction before sides, all passing right arm to right.

Turn ladies with left hand and dance on to lady who was on right of gent's original position.

Turn this lady with right hand.

Gents now cross to opposite ladies with their left hand, tops a fraction before sides as before.

Turn the lady with their left hand and pass on to own partner.

Turn partner with right hand once in place.

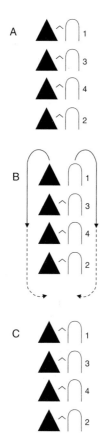

(D) Swing into Line

(a) Leading tops half-turn in place to face outward from the circle; at the same time the other couples swing into line behind leading tops. Line-up should be 1-3-4-2.

(b) Partners of leading couple 1 turn outward from each other, gent to left, lady to right, and Lead Around to place vacated by opposite tops couple 2. Gents follow leading gent, and ladies follow leading lady.

c) Partners of the leading couple turn in towards each other and taking hands lead up to place, being followed in like manner by the other three couples.

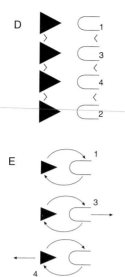

(d) Release hands, all half-turn inwards to face partners, dance Rising Step on both feet.

(e) Partners now take hands and dance clockwise into original position.

(E) Set All-Round

(a) Partners take right hands and turn half-round. Gents, retaining partners' hands, take left hand of lady on left so that gents are now all facing outwards, ladies facing inwards. All dance Rising Step. Release right hands, gents turn around lady on left, return to own partner with right hand and turn once in place.

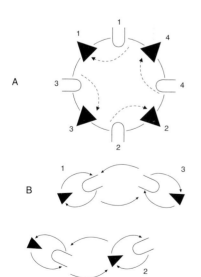

(b) Leading tops and leading sides dance around each other while opposite tops and opposite sides do likewise. The Body ends

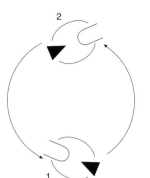

(F) First Figure –

Advance and Retire

Leading and opposite tops advance and retire twice.
Both couples then dance a complete circle around each
other.

When both tops and sides have performed the Figure,
repeat the Body.

(G) Second Figure –

Gent gives right hand to opposite lady.
Both move forward in a semi-circle, gents clockwise,
ladies anti-clockwise.
Continue to meet partner with left hand then opposite
lady with right hand, and on to own partner with left
hand to finish in position.
Gents of leading and opposite tops advance to opposite
lady and give her right hand.
Turn once in place and then return to partner with his
left hand and turn in place.
Both gents advance to centre, take right hands, turn once
and advance to opposite lady.
Give her left hand and turn once in place, return to own
partner and take partner's hands.
Top couples now dance a complete circle around each
other anti-clockwise back to place.
Leading and opposite sides now dance the Figure.

On completion of the Figure, repeat the Body.

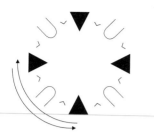

(H) Finish

All dancers join hands in a circle.

Advance to centre and retire, again advance to centre and retire.

All side step anti-clockwise and finish with two Rising Steps.

All side step back clockwise ending with two Rising Steps.

All advance and retire twice to centre.

All side step clockwise ending with two Rising Steps.

All now side step back to place ending with two Rising Steps.

Each couple now takes hands and swings around anti-clockwise to finish dance.

(Note: At social dances, couples swing in place to end dance.)

The Three Tunes

This is an Eight-Hand Figure Dance from County Armagh.

Music – Danced to three tunes: 'Haste to the Wedding', 'Leslie's Hornpipe', and 'The German Beau'. The reel is taken at a rather slower pace than a jig, and the hornpipe slightly slower still. There is no stop between the various tunes.
Movements A–B and in the repeat G–H are danced to the jig tune.
Movements C–D and I–J are danced to the hornpipe.
Movements E–F and K–L are danced in reel time.

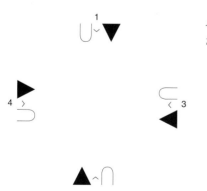

Formation – Eight dancers (four couples) in a ring holding hands.

Dance Movements

A. Sides	=	16 Bars
B. Rings	=	8 Bars
C. Lead Around	=	16 Bars
D. Stamp and Clap	=	16 Bars
E. See-Saw	=	16 Bars
F. Roly-Poly	=	24 Bars
G. Hook and Chain	=	16 Bars
H. Rings	=	16 Bars
I. Sides under Arms	=	16 Bars
J. Stamp and Clap	=	16 Bars
K. Thread the Needle	=	16 Bars
L. Roly-Poly	=	24 Bars

(A) Sides

All dance side step to left (clockwise), finishing with two Short Threes, all side step to the right (anti-clockwise) finishing with two Short Threes, all side step to the right (anti-clockwise) ending with two Threes, all side step to the left (clockwise) ending with two Threes.

While doing the last two Threes, all couples release hands and fall back to places.

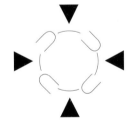

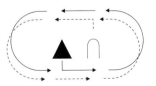

(B) Rings

The four ladies advance to centre, take hands, and with four Promenade Steps, dance round clockwise to places; all clap hands twice.

Partners dance half side step (1-2-3) past each other, gents passing behind to the right.

They now side step back to places, ladies passing behind. The four gents now advance to centre, take hands, and with four Promenade Steps, dance round clockwise to places.

All clap hands twice; partners dance (right 1-2-3, back to left 1-2-3-4-5-7) half side step (1-2-3) past each other, gents passing behind to the right.

They now side step back to places, ladies passing behind.

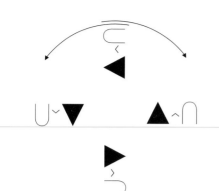

(C) Lead Around

Dancers take hands.

Gent holds lady's left in his right, half-right turn and dance anti-clockwise around with eight Promenade Steps in a complete circle.

They then release hands, about turn inwards, gent takes partner's right hand in his left.

They all then dance eight Promenade Steps clockwise back to their starting position.

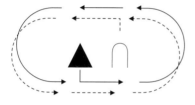

(D) Stamp and Clap

All dancers stamp first the right foot, then the left, and then the right again, to one bar of music.

Clap hands together three times on second bar.

Side step past each other, the gent passing behind, and side step back to places, the gent now passing in front. Clap alternate hands five times quickly on legs above knees, commencing with right hand on right knee. Clap hands together three times.

All dancers again stamp first the right foot, then the left, and then the right again, to one bar of music.

Clap hands together three times on second bar.

Side step past each other, the gent passing behind, and side step back to places, the gent now passing in front. Clap alternate hands five times quickly on legs above knees, commencing with right hand on right knee. Clap hands together three times.

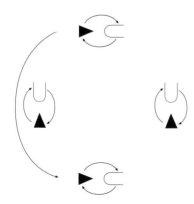

(E) See-Saw

All couples face their partners, take uncrossed hands, and dance around (revolving clockwise) in an anti-clockwise direction until they reach their starting position.

Couples now return clockwise, revolving in an anti-clockwise direction until they return to their original position.

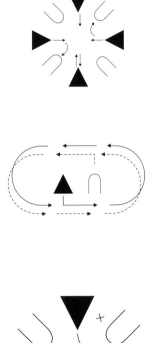

(F) Roly-Poly

All dancers hold closed hands at chest level and roll them round each other in a forward direction (1 bar), and then roll them back in the opposite direction (1 bar); pivot once to right on right heel (1 bar); clap hands together once (1 bar).

Gents shake right fist forward in air once (in threatening manner), hand about shoulder level, at the same time placing right foot forward on ground, bringing it back as hand is returned to side (1 bar).

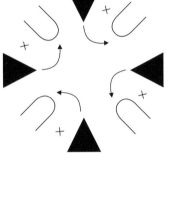

Shake left fist in similar manner, placing left foot forward (1 bar); stamp feet three times (1 bar); clap hands together three times towards partner (1 bar).Partners side step past each other and back to places (4 bars).

Repeat (F).

(G) Hook and Chain

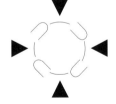

Each gent hooks left arm of lady on left in his left, turning her once in place, chains back to partner, taking her right hand in his right, and continues the chain movement, giving alternate hands to each lady in turn until all return to places.

(H) Rings

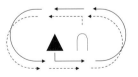

The four ladies advance to centre, take hands, and with four Promenade Steps, dance round clockwise to places. All clap hands twice.

Partners dance half side step (1-2-3) past each other, gents passing behind to the right.

They now side step back to places, ladies passing behind. The four gents now advance to centre, take hands, and with four Promenade Steps, dance round clockwise to places. All clap hands twice.

Partners dance (right 1-2-3, back to left 1-2-3-4-5-7) half side step (1-2-3) past each other, gents passing behind to the right.

They now side step back to places, ladies passing behind.

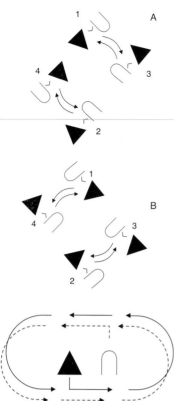

(I) Sides under Arms (Arches)

Partners take inside hands, top couples holding up hands to form an arch.

With Promenade Step, tops and sides change places, first sides passing under arch of first tops, while second sides pass under that of second tops.

Release hands and face about.

All take inside hands again and dance back to places, this time sides making arch and tops passing underneath.

The above movement is now repeated, this time tops make an arch and dance to side couple on their right, release hands and dance back to place, and side couples make the arch and tops dance under.

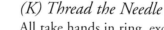

(J) Stamp and Clap

All dancers stamp first the right foot, then the left, and then the right again, to one bar of music.

Clap hands together three times on second bar.

Side step past each other, the gent passing behind, and side step back to places, the gent now passing in front.

Clap alternate hands five times quickly on legs above knees, commencing with right hand on right knee. Clap hands together three times.

All dancers again stamp first the right foot, then the left, and then the right again, to one bar of music.

Clap hands together three times on second bar.

Side step past each other, the gent passing behind, and side step back to places, the gent now passing in front.

Clap alternate hands five times quickly on legs above knees, commencing with right hand on right knee. Clap hands together three times.

(K) Thread the Needle

All take hands in ring, except gent of first tops and lady of first sides.

Lady of first sides leads the other dancers with the Promenade Step, under the raised hands of couple on her right and takes all the other dancers of the line after her, and so back to places.

Repeat this movement. This time gent of first tops now leads the other dancers, passing under the arch made by the couple on his left first sides.

All dance back to places.

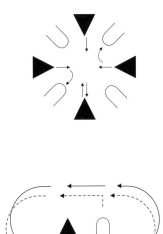

(L) Roly-Poly

All dancers hold closed hands at chest level and roll them round each other in a forward direction (1 bar), and then roll them back in the opposite direction (1 bar), pivot once to right on right heel (1 bar), clap hands together once (1 bar).

Gents shake right fist forward in air once (in threatening manner), hand about shoulder level, at the same time placing right foot forward on ground, bringing it back as hand is returned to side (1 bar); shake left fist in similar manner, placing left foot forward (1 bar); stamp feet three times (1 bar); clap hands together three times towards partner (1 bar).

Partners side step past each other and back to places (4 bars).

Repeat movement.

Morris Reel

Music – Reels.

Formation – Four couples in a square.

Steps – Side Step, Promenade Step, Threes.

Dance Movements

A. Lead Around	= 16 Bars
B. Sides	= 16 Bars
C. Right Hands Across	= 32 Bars
D. Return Chain	= 16 Bars
E. Back to Back	= 16 Bars
F. First Figure	= 16 Bars
G. Second Figure	= 16 Bars
H. Finish	= 40 Bars

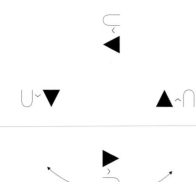

(A) Lead Around

Dancers take hands.

Gent holds lady's left in his right, half-right turn and dance anti-clockwise around with eight Promenade Steps in a complete circle.

They then release hands, about turn inwards.

Gent takes partner's right hand in his left.

They all then dance eight Promenade Steps clockwise back to their starting position.

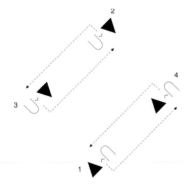

The Body

(B) Sides

Partners take hands, right hand in right, left hand in left. Leading and opposite tops side step to the right to the positions occupied by their contrary couples, while leading and opposite sides side step to the left to position of their contrary couples, all ending with two Short Threes.

All side step back to place, ending with two Short Threes. Tops now side step to the left in front while sides side step to the right behind, ending with two Short Threes. All side step back to place, ending with two Short Threes.

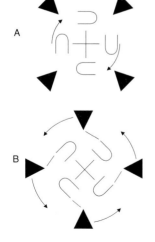

(C) Right Hands Across

Ladies give right hands across in the centre, dance round clockwise; reverse, giving left hands across, and dance back to place.

Retain hands, give right hand to partner's right, lead around, and turn once into place.

Gents now do likewise.

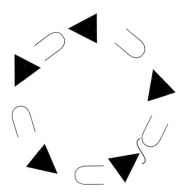

(D) Return Chain

Gents are now in original position, holding partner's right hand in own right.

Couples face each other and start to chain, gents give left hand to lady on right, ladies give left hand to gents on left; all chain around giving right and left hand alternately until meeting own partner again with right hand at opposite side of the circle.

Halfway round: turn right around partner and chain back to original position, meeting partner with right hand and turning in place.

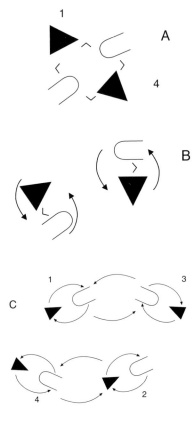

E) Back to Back

Gent, holding partner's right hand, side steps towards the left of contrary lady, while partner dances towards the left of contrary (couple on right of top couple) gent.

Gent then takes left hand of contrary lady while partner takes left hand of contrary gent, the four dancers now forming a circle, gents being back to back, ladies facing each other.

All dance two Short Threes.

Gent releases partner's right hand, turns around contrary lady and returns to own partner, passing other gent right arm to right.

Partners take both hands and dance around couple opposite to contrary couple (couple on the left side of top couple) and back to place.

The Body ends

The Haymakers Jig – Long Dance

This is one of the most popular Irish social dances. It is similar in formation and movement to the American dance The Virginia Reel, and the Scottish dance Strip The Willow.

Music – Double jig time.

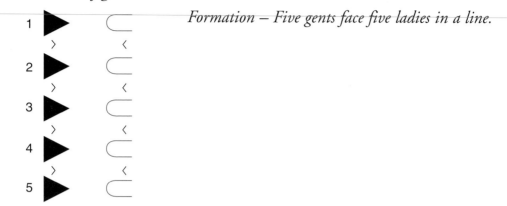

Formation – Five gents face five ladies in a line.

Steps – Rising Step, Promenade Step.

Dance Movements		
	A. Advance and Retire	= 16 Bars
	B. Turn in Centre	= 16 Bars
	C. Swing in Centre	= 16 Bars
	D. Link Arms	= 24 Bars
	E. Arch	= 8 Bars

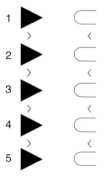

(A) Advance and Retire

The lines of dancers advance towards each other with Promenade Step, and retire to places.

They advance and retire once again.

All now dance Rising Step on right foot, and then on the left foot.

All advance and retire once more.

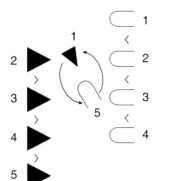

(B) Turn in Centre

Gent of first couple and lady of last couple advance with Promenade Step to meet in centre, and taking right hands, turn once and dance back to places.

Gent of last couple and lady of first couple now advance to centre and taking right hand turn once and dance back to place.

Gent of first couple and lady of last couple advance with Promenade Step to meet in centre, and taking left hands, turn once and dance back to places.

Gent of last couple and lady of first couple now advance to centre and taking left hands turn once and dance back to place.

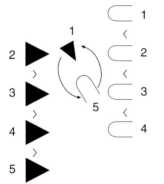

(C) Swing in Centre

Gent of first couple and lady of last couple now advance again to centre, but this time they take both hands, crossed, and swing around clockwise, before retiring to place.

Gent of last couple and lady of first couple now advance to centre, they take both hands, crossed, and swing around clockwise, before retiring to place.

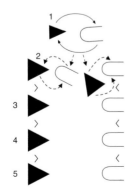

(D) Link Arms (Chain)

The lady and gent of the first couple advance to meet, link right arms and turn once.

Then they smoothly dance on to second couple, the gent linking left arms with the second lady, and the lady linking left arm with the second gent, and again pass back to partner.

The leading couple link right arms again and turn once and pass on to the third couple whom they turn, and so on until they have danced with the last couple.

The first couple now take hands and swing down the centre to original places.

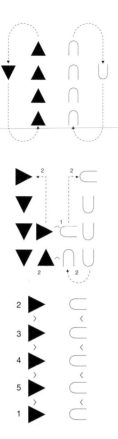

(E) Arch

The gent and lady of the first couple now turn outwards and march along outside their respective lines, followed by each line of dancers – gents follow gents and ladies follow ladies until they come to the end of the set (last couple's position).

Then they face each other and hold both hands above, uncrossed, to form an arch.

The other couples meet in turn, and taking inside hands pass under arch and back along the line of the dance, till couple 2 – having released hands – occupy the place of couple 1, couple 3 being in the place of couple 2, and so on.

The original leading couple now fall into line in the place of the last couple, and all are now in line to recommence dance in the new position.

The dance is repeated until each couple has had the opportunity to become the leading couple in the line.

Lannigan's Ball – Round Dance

Music – Danced to the tune of the same name in single jig time.

Formation – Six couples in a ring.

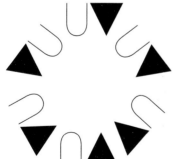

Steps – Promenade Step, Rise and Grind.

Dance Movements		
	A. Ring	= 16 Bars
	B. Quarters Hook	= 8 Bars
	C. Rise and Grind	= 16 Bars
	D. Lead Around in Centre	= 16 Bars
	E. Flirtation	= 16 Bars

F. Stack-up   = 16 Bars
G. Lead Around   = 8 Bars

(A) Ring

All dancers take hands in a circle.

All dance eight Promenade Steps clockwise, still holding hands.

All dancers turn right and dance eight Promenade Steps anti-clockwise.

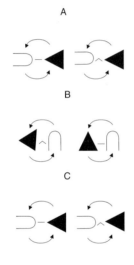

A

B

C

(B) Quarters Hook

Gents link right arms with the lady on their left, and dancing the Promenade Step dance around the lady and back to partner with left arm.

Continue the chain movement back to the lady on the left with right hand and back to partner, each lady and gent finishing facing the lady or gent in the next position; for example, gents face left ladies' right.

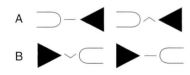

A

B

(C) Rise and Grind

In their present position all dance the Rise and Grind on the right foot (2 bars); repeat on the left foot (2 bars); continue with one throw right (1 bar) and one throw left (1 bar); and finish with the Rise and Grind on the right foot (2 bars).

On the last Grind (1-2-3-4 movement), all turn to face partners and repeat Rise and Grind on the left foot (2 bars). Repeat on the right foot (2 bars); continue with one throw left (1 bar) and one throw right (1 bar) ending with the Rise and Grind on the right foot (2 bars).

Finish facing centre.

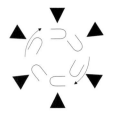

(D) Lead Around in Centre

Gents stand in position while ladies dance three Promenade Steps clockwise in the centre.

On the fourth step they all turn right about, and dance back to place anti-clockwise to partner who they turn with the right hand into centre, the ladies getting into stationary positions.

The gents now dance around in the centre as the ladies did, but the gents dance anti-clockwise and return clockwise turning partner with right hand into place.

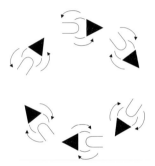

(E) Flirtation

All dancers face partners and take two hands uncrossed and swing once in place (2 bars).

Gents now dance on to the next lady on their right, turning each one in place with hands uncrossed until they reach their own partners.

When the gents reach their own partners, they end up with their backs to the centre facing their partners.

(F) Stack-up

While gents clap in rhythm (2 claps to a bar), ladies dance around them clockwise with six Promenade Steps. On the seventh and eighth step, the ladies, having completed a circle, give both hands to their partner and turn their partners out, leaving the ladies with their backs to the centre (8 bars).

This movement is now repeated by the gents, while the ladies clap hands; the gents also dance clockwise on the last two steps,

The gents give both hands to their partners and turn into Lead Around position.

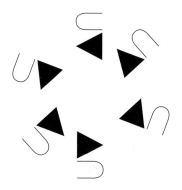

(G) Lead Around

All dancers now dance eight Promenade Steps anti-clockwise finishing in opening position.

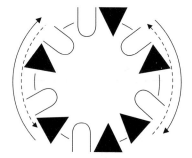

(H) Ring

All dancers take hands in a circle.
All dance eight Promenade Steps clockwise, still holding hands.
All dancers turn right and dance eight Promenade Steps anti-clockwise.

The Sixteen-Hand Reel

Music – Reels.

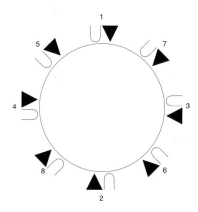

Formation – Eight Couples in a Circle.

1 and 2 = first tops
3 and 4 = first sides
5 and 6 = second tops
7 and 8 = second sides

Steps – Side Step, Promenade Step, Short Threes.

Dance Movements

A. Lead Around	= 16 Bars
B. Sides	= 8 Bars
C. Hands Round	= 8 Bars
D. Sides	= 8 Bars
E. Hands Round	= 8 Bars
F. Half Chain	= 16 Bars
G. Link Arms	= 16 Bars
H. First Figure	= 16 Bars
I. Second Figure	= 24 Bars
J. Third Figure	= 16 Bars
K. Finish	= 40 Bars

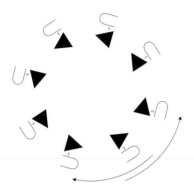

(A) Lead Around
Dancers take hands.
Gent holds lady's left hand in his right, half-right turn
and dance anti-clockwise around with eight Promenade
Steps in a complete circle.
They then release hands, about turn inwards.
Gent takes partner's right hand in his left.
They all then dance eight Promenade Steps clockwise
back to their starting position.

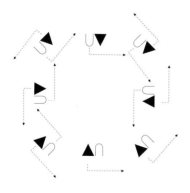

The Body
(B) Sides
Gents side step behind partner while ladies side step in
front of partner ending with two Short Threes.
The couples now side step back to place.
This time the ladies dance behind and the gents in front,
ending with two Short Threes.

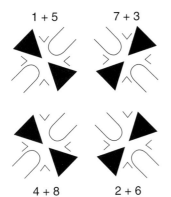

1 + 5   7 + 3

4 + 8   2 + 6

(C) Hands Round

Leading and opposite tops and leading and opposite sides each form a ring with the couple on their right by joining hands, shoulder high.

All side step to the left (clockwise), ending with two Short Threes.

The rings now side step back to the right anti-clockwise, ending with two Short Threes.

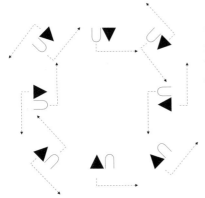

(D) Sides

Gents side step behind partner while ladies side step in front of partner ending with two Short Threes.

The couples now side step back to place.

This time the ladies dance behind and the gents in front, ending with two Short Threes.

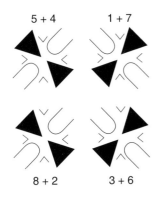

5 + 4   1 + 7

8 + 2   3 + 6

(E) Hands Round

Leading and opposite tops and leading and opposite sides each form a ring with the couple on their left by joining hands, shoulder high.

All side step to the left (clockwise), ending with two Short Threes.

The rings now side step back to the right, anti-clockwise, ending with two Short Threes.

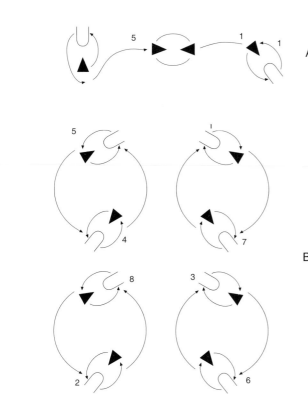

(F) Half Chain

All take partner's right hand, half-right turn.
Gents move anti-clockwise, ladies move clockwise.
Gents give left hand to the lady who was on his right,
and ladies give left hand to gent who was on her left.
They all advance to meet the oncoming dancers, giving
right and left hand alternately until meeting own partner.
With right hand in position opposite starting position,
each couple now take both hands, crossed, right in right
and left in left and lead round to place in the direction
the gent was dancing, anti-clockwise.

G) Link Arms

A Gents of leading and opposite tops and leading and opposite sides advance to the gents
on their right and take right arm, inner sides
of forearms touching (Hook).

Dance around each other clockwise, release
arms and advance to meet the partner of the
gent.

Give her left hand, dance around her and
return to place.

Gents, passing right shoulder to right
shoulder, give right hand to partner and
B turn once in place.

Partners take hands and dance a complete
circle back to place around the couple with
whom they danced the second Ring – see
(E) above for example – couples 1 and 7
around each other as do couples 2 and 8, 3
and 6, 4 and 5.

The Body ends

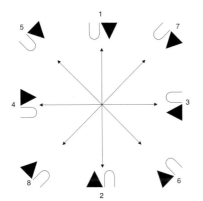

(H) First Figure – Advance and Retire

Leading and opposite tops advance with two Promenade Steps (2 bars) to the centre and retire with two Promenade Steps (2 bars). They repeat this movement once again. Both couples then dance complete circle around each other anti-clockwise back to starting position. Leading and opposite sides now dance the Figure followed by second tops and finally by second sides.

Repeat the Body.

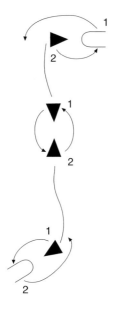

(I) Second Figure – Right Hand to Opposite Lady

Gents of leading and opposite tops advance with Promenade Step to the lady opposite and give her their right hand; turn once in place.

Gents now return to own partner and give her their left hand; turn once in place.

Both gents advance to centre and take right hands and turn once.

They then advance to the opposite ladies and give her their left hand and turn once in place.

They then return to their own partner, take both hands, and both couples dance around each other anti-clockwise.

Leading and opposite sides next dance the Figure followed by second tops and finally by second sides.
Repeat the Body.

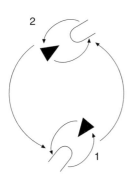

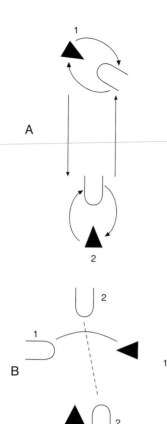

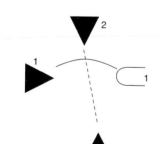

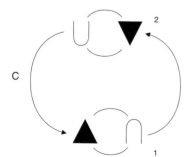

(J) Third Figure – Arch Arms

Leading and opposite tops take both partners' hands, crossed, right in right, left in left, and dance a complete turn into the centre (2 bars).

Leading tops release left hands, raise right hands to form an arch, allowing opposite lady to pass through (2 bars); half-turn and allow opposite gent to pass through the arch (2 bars).

Partners now take both hands and dance a complete turn to opposite couples original place (2 bars).

Again dance into centre (2 bars).

This time opposite tops release left hands, raise right hands, make an arch and allow the leading lady to pass through (2 bars); half-turn and allow leading gent to pass through (2 bars).

Partners take hands and dance back to place (2 bars).

Remaining couples then perform the Figure in the same order as previous figures.

Repeat the Body.

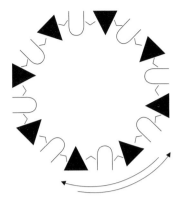

K) Finish

All dancers join hands in the circle, forearms bent sharply upwards, elbows held in to the sides.

Advance to the centre and retire.

Advance again and retire.

All side step right (anti-clockwise) and finish with two Short Threes.

All side step back to left (clockwise) ending with two Short Threes.

Advance and retire twice as before.

All side step left (clockwise) ending with two Short Threes and side step back to the right (anti-clockwise), ending with two Short Threes.

Each couple take both hands and swing around to the right and finish off.